Coline Serreau

MANCHESTER
UNIVERSITY PRESS

French Film Directors

DIANA HOLMES and ROBERT INGRAM *series editors*
DUDLEY ANDREWS *series consultant*

Luc Besson   SUSAN HAYWARD

Diane Kurys   CARRIE TARR

François Truffaut   DIANA HOLMES AND ROBERT INGRAM

Agnès Varda   ALISON SMITH

forthcoming titles

Jean-Jacques Beineix   PHIL POWRIE

Bertrand Blier   SUE HARRIS

Robert Bresson   KEITH READER

Claude Chabrol   GUY AUSTIN

Jean-Luc Godard   STEVE CANNON and ELIANE MEYER

George Méliès   ELIZABETH EZRA

Jean Renoir   MARTIN O'SHAUGHNESSY

Eric Rohmer   HOWARD DAVIES

FRENCH FILM DIRECTORS

Coline Serreau

BRIGITTE ROLLET

Manchester University Press

MANCHESTER AND NEW YORK

distributed exclusively in the USA by St. Martin's Press

Published by Manchester University Press
Oxford Road, Manchester M13 9NR, UK
and Room 400, 175 Fifth Avenue, New York, NY 10010, USA

Distributed exclusively in the USA by
St. Martin's Press, Inc., 175 Fifth Avenue, New York,
NY 10010, USA

Distributed exclusively in Canada by
UBC Press, University of British Columbia, 6344 Memorial Road,
Vancouver, BC, Canada V6T 1Z2

British Library Cataloguing-in-Publication Data
A catalogue record for this book is available from the British Library

Library of Congress Cataloging-in-Publication Data applied for

ISBN 0 7190 5087 1 *hardback*
     0 7190 5088 X *paperback*

First published 1998

05 04 03 02 01 00 99 98   10 9 8 7 6 5 4 3 2 1

Typeset in Scala with Meta display
by Koinonia, Manchester
Printed in Great Britain
by Biddles Limited, Guildford and King's Lynn

Contents

List of plates

All stills courtesy of BFI Stills, Posters and Designs

Series editors' foreword

To an anglophone audience, the combination of the words 'French' and 'cinema' evokes a particular kind of film: elegant and wordy, sexy but serious – an image as dependent upon national stereotypes as is that of the crudely commercial Hollywood block-buster, which is not to say that either image is without foundation. Over the past two decades, this generalised sense of a significant relationship between French identity and film has been explored in scholarly books and articles, and has entered the curriculum at university level and, in Britain, at high-school level. The study of film as art-form and (to a lesser extent) as industry, has become a popular and widespread element of French Studies, and French cinema has acquired an important place within Film Studies. Meanwhile, the growth in multi-screen and 'art-house' cinemas, together with the development of the video industry, has led to the greater availability of foreign-language films to an English-speaking audience. Responding to these developments, this series is designed for students and teachers seeking information and accessible but rigorous critical study of French cinema, and for the enthusiastic filmgoer who wants to know more.

The adoption of a director-based approach raises questions about *auteurism*. A series that catagorises films not according to period or to genre (for example), but to the person who directed them, runs the risk of espousing a romantic view of film as the product of solitary inspiration. On this model, the critic's role might seem to be that of discovering continuities, revealing a

necessarily coherent set of themes and motifs which correspond
to the particular genius of the individual. This is not our aim: the
auteur perspective of film, itself most clearly articulated in France
in the early 1950s, will be interrogated in certain volumes of the
series, and throughout, the director will be treated as one highly
significant element in a complex process of film production and
reception which includes socio-economic and political determinants,
the work of a large and highly skilled team of artists and
technicians, the mechanisms of production and distribution, and
the complex and multiply determined responses of spectators.

The work of some of the directors in the series is already well
known outside France, that of others is less so – the aim is both to
provide informative and original English-language studies of
established figures, and to extend the range of French directors
known to anglophone students of cinema. We intend the series to
contribute to the promotion of the formal and informal study of
French films, and to the pleasure of those who watch them.

DIANA HOLMES
ROBERT INGRAM

Acknowledgements

I would like to thank the members of my department at the University of Portsmouth for their support during the writing of this book. I am also grateful to my research group, the Francophone Area Studies, for their financial support which enabled me to obtain teaching relief and to travel to France for my research. I also thank my students for their challenges and ideas.

I would also like to acknowledge the help of Martin Evans, Eleanor Steward-Richardson and Alasdair King in the reading of my prose, and more especially of Christine Bard for her unlimited support, her wide knowledge of French feminism and her invaluable suggestions.

My special thanks go to the series editors Diana Holmes and Robert Ingram who made extremely helpful comments at all stages of the writing. Others whom I should like to thank include Carrie Tarr and Susan Hayward.

Finally I am very grateful to Coline Serreau for taking time to meet me, and to her assistant Colette Sonnier for her help in providing useful information.

Dedicated to my parents Anne and Yves Rollet, and my sisters and brothers, Pascale, Bruno, Claire, Jean-François, Béatrice and Agnès

List of abbreviations

CNC	Centre National du Cinéma
FEMIS	Formation et Enseignement pour les Métiers de l'Image et du Son
FIFF	Festival International de Film de Femmes
FR3	France Région 3 (Third French channel), France 3
IDHEC	Institut des Hautes Etudes Cinématographiques
INA	Institut National de l'Audiovisuel
MLAC	Mouvement pour la Libération de l'Avortement et de la Contraception
MLF	Mouvement de Libération des Femmes
ORTF	Office de Radiodiffusion–Télévision Française
PCF	Parti Communiste Français
PS	Parti Socialiste
RAI	Radio Italiana
RMI	Revenu Minimum d'Insertion
TF1	Télévision Française 1

Introduction

Coline Serreau's career makes her in many respects a typical 'product of her time'. A strong believer in 1970s' ideologies and ideas such as Marxism and feminism, she directed her first two films in the mid- and late 1970s, and reflected not only the concerns of the decade, but also the cinematographic choices made by many filmmakers – and more especially women – of the time. A decade later, and at a time of collapsing ideologies – culminating with the fall of the Berlin wall in 1989 – her interests seem to switch slightly away from post-May '68 agendas to more consensual 1980s' topics and filmic genres. Twenty years after making a documentary which is still hailed as *the* feminist documentary *par excellence*, she came back with her latest film so far – *La Belle Verte*, released in France in September 1996 – to 1970s' preoccupations such as ecology and the defence of the environment via a science fiction tale, with a typically 1990s' flavour. Although she shares similarities with other French female filmmakers who started their career in the 1970s, hers is in many ways unique, and it could be said that throughout her career she has skilfully mixed tradition and innovation, in topics as well as in very personal rewriting of existing narrative forms.

The first chapter of this book is devoted not only to some relevant biographical aspects of Coline Serreau's personal and artistic life, but also to the social, historical and political context of her debut. Since the beginning, she has seemed to follow different trends and traditions which are central to both French cinema and women's films in particular. However, her main attribute is to 'confuse' the issue by making *auteur* films as well as commercial films, and by constantly mixing cinematographic genres within the same narrative. Her constant 'borrowing' from varied narrative genres, together with the recurrent topical elements of her films, are analysed to illustrate this aspect. In order to grasp the very specific mood of France in the late 1960s, the major social and historical turning point, the 'revolution' of May '68, is briefly presented. Significant issues related to this event, such as social movements, women's rights and the sexual revolution, are addressed. The characteristics and tendencies of post-1968 French cinema and the changing perception of culture overall and films in particular are also discussed. This leads to an analysis of the different ways women fit into this new cinematographic land-scape, on both sides of the camera.

The second chapter deals with the 1970s' flavour of Serreau's work (film and drama) and more especially with the importance of politics. After a brief introduction on French political films and on the specificities of 1970s' French documentaries in this regard, *Mais qu'est-ce qu'elles veulent?*, Serreau's most committed film to date, is analysed. The recurrent double axis in Serreau's work, that of class and gender, is also examined. The element of utopia, which is typical of numerous 1970s' texts and has strongly inspired Serreau's career, is not the only influence to be found in her work. Ideas and genres related to seventeenth- and more especially eighteenth-century French literature are also an obvious inspiration.

Taking intertextuality in its broadest sense, Chapter 3 will assess the strong literary influence on the tone, genre and content of Serreau's films and dramas. Fairy-tales and philosophical tales, together with the social and political satire characteristic of seven-teenth- and eighteenth-century French literature, are combined with a 1970s' flavour by the director-dramatist who addresses issues of gender and race which were not on the agenda of the male French writers of previous centuries. While their texts suggested a direct or indirect 'moral' in accordance with their time's concerns, Serreau offers a modern version of the seventeenth-century

French moralists tinged with eighteenth-century use of humour.

The fourth chapter is devoted to another major aspect of Serreau's creation and is concerned with the cinematographic genres she uses. In this regard as in others, her choices could be seen as in accordance with the main tendencies of French cinema as a whole, as well as the French cinema of the 1970s and 1980s. This chapter deals mainly with a description and an analysis of Serreau's comedies, within the wider perspective of French comedies (or *comédies à la française*). The aim is to show to what extent her comedies both reproduce and reject the usual and typical 'ingredients' of the genre. The specificity (or the lack of specificity) of French comedies in general is also considered. After a presentation of the genre, which is one of the most popular in France, the issue of its traditionally male-centred humour and joke-making is addressed. The possibilities of women's reappropriation of laughter is then considered before Serreau's humour is examined in more detail. Keeping in mind the success of Serreau's comedies abroad (leading to an American remake of *Trois hommes et un couffin* (1985)), this chapter will also suggest an analysis of national versus universal humour.

The fifth – and last – chapter deals with the element of 'family' or community which is recurrent in Serreau's films and plays. Issues related to sexual and gender roles are explored and the ubiquitous maternal figure is put in the wider perspective of France's long tradition of family policies. French feminists' sometimes uneasy concern with such a complex issue, and the numerous 'solutions' they have advocated since the early 1900s, are also presented in order to underline Serreau's tradition and novelty in this field.

1

Coline Serreau, May '68 and the 1970s in France

It runs in the family: Serreau's family background

Coline Serreau is one of the most famous female French directors alive, not only in France but also abroad. She is the only woman with a film figuring in the list of the twenty most popular French movies since the start of the Fifth Republic (1958), reaching fourth position with *Trois hommes et un couffin*.

Coline Serreau was born in Paris on 29 October 1947, the daughter of Geneviève Serreau (1915–1981), a writer and translator, and of Jean-Marie Serreau (1915–1973), a stage director considered by some as one of the most important of the 1950s, whose works include *inter alia* stage adaptations of Samuel Beckett, Jean Genet, Aimé Césaire and Eugène Ionesco. Both her parents had been resisters during the Second World War and were left-wing political activists. Her mother was among the 121 writers and artists who in 1960 signed the 'déclaration sur le droit à l'insoumission en Algérie',[1] which defended the right of soldiers to refuse to do their military service in Algeria.

In 1952, Geneviève and Jean-Marie Serreau created the Théâtre de Babylone where the theatrical avant-garde met. As far as their work was concerned, they were in many regards innovators in their respective fields. Her mother was the first translator of Bertolt Brecht and shared her taste for discovering new talents (such as the novelist Georges Perec and the playwright Francisco

---

1 'Declaration for the right to avoid the draft'.

Arrabal) with her daughter. Her father was a former pupil of Charles Dullin, an actor-director whose name is closely linked with the Front Populaire (Popular Front, 1936–37) and the *théâtre populaire* (theatre of the people). It was Dullin's report for the Front Populaire about the state of theatre in the provinces which initiated a series of state-led innovations in theatre, amongst these the creation of the Centre Dramatiques Nationaux in the late 1940s.

Jean-Marie Serreau was actually the stage director who made Beckett, Genet and Ionesco's plays known and available to French theatre-goers. His desire for cultural experiments was wide-ranging and included contemporary music as well as video long before they became fashionable. Serreau often emphasises in her interviews the bohemian lifestyle of her parents, and the effect of this on her childhood. On the one hand she inhabited the privileged cultural environment where playwrights who would later become world famous, such as Beckett or Ionesco, would often come to her parents' house, and on the other hand in material terms the household was far from privileged. Serreau often underlines her family's lack of financial resources. The community-like atmosphere of the Serreau household when Coline was in her teens can be found in many of her films (see Chapters 3 and 5). The family tie between Serreau and her brothers Nicolas and Dominique is also obvious from the very beginning of her career. She toured with the latter in the year of her *baccalauréat* and both her brothers have played parts in her films and plays.

Coline Serreau studied music at the famous Conservatoire of the rue Blanche in Paris together with modern and classical dance. She also trained as an acrobat and specialised in the trapeze. This artistic versatility probably explains the extreme variety and the multifaceted nature of her career. Her latest film so far – *La Belle Verte*, released in France in September 1996 – epitomises this as she not only directed it, but also played the leading part, indulging in the last sequences in some trapeze exercises, and wrote the music soundtrack.

She started her acting career as a theatre actress and musician in the late 1960s. In 1970 she played the leading role in *L'Escalier de Silas*. Very early, she pursued acting (on stage, for television and cinema) and writing simultaneously. In 1971 she collaborated with the radical stand-up comedian Coluche in both the writing and the acting of the show *Thérèse est triste*, performing mainly in the fringe cabaret setting of the *café-théâtres* which flourished in Paris at the time thanks in large part to their iconoclastic humour. At the same time, she was acting for television and cinema, sometimes writing the script and/or the dialogues such as in Jean-Louis Bertuccelli's film *On s'est trompé d'histoire d'amour* released in France in 1974 (see the filmography and below for more details). In 1975 she made her debut as a film director. She directed a short fiction film, entitled *Le Rendez-vous*, for the second French public channel.

From feminist activist documentary to mainstream comedies: genres and mixture of genres

In an interview in February 1977,[2] Coline Serreau told the journalist who asked her whether she would continue to make documentaries that 'j'ai envie de continuer la fiction aussi, et j'ai envie de continuer à jouer: pour moi, tout cela c'est la même chose ... La fiction est un moyen essentiel pour dire d'autres choses à un autre moment. Je peux revenir à l'un comme à l'autre. Et je peux revenir au théâtre parce que c'est un des rares moments, un des seuls moments où on apprend vraiment à communiquer avec le public'[3] (Serreau 1978a: 5). This statement could easily summarise Serreau's career twenty years on. She has remained faithful to the artistic versatility she so valued at her cinematographic debut, and has always refused to be restricted to a specific genre. This chapter

---

2 Published only in April–May 1978, that is, a few months after the release of her first films – one documentary and one fiction film – as a director.

3 'I want to continue with fiction as well, and I want to continue with acting: for me it's all the same ... Fiction is an essential way to say other things at other moments. I can move from one to the other. I can come back on stage because drama is one of the rare moments, one of the only moments, when one learns to communicate with the audience.'

will therefore present the director's films in chronological order and situate them in their political, social and cultural context. It will examine as well the different genres and narratives from one film to the next, and show how they illustrate various aspects of Serreau's art: first the wide variety of her cinematographic skills and influences, and secondly the multiple means she used and still uses both to entertain and to make her audience think. The way her films epitomise the evolution of French cinema and society in the last twenty years will also be considered.

From acting and scriptwriting to directing

Serreau's early career is typical of many of her female contemporaries. Although a few older female filmmakers (such as Agnès Varda, Marguerite Duras and Nelly Kaplan) managed to make films in the 1960s (even late 1950s for Varda), most of the baby boomers became directors only in the 1970s. They often started with acting and felt, as numerous actresses did at the time, either a growing frustration with the roles they were offered and/or an intense desire to make their own films. As will be seen in the next chapter, there was a long way between their initial desire and the actual realisation of their first feature film. The intermediate step between acting and directing was often scriptwriting. Coline Serreau did both as she played the leading female part in the filmic adaptation of her first script directed by Jean-Louis Bertuccelli in 1974, *On s'est trompé d'histoire d'amour*. As will be shown later, this film dealt with a lot of women's and women's movements' concerns at the time, such as unwanted pregnancy and contraception. It also illustrates Coline Serreau's attention to issues which affected her whole cinematographic career, whatever genre she used, and which are closely linked to May '68 and the different social movements that followed.

Promising directing debut: *Mais qu'est-ce qu'elles veulent?* and *Pourquoi pas!* (1975–1978)

The mid-1970s represent a key moment in the history of women and filmmaking in France as more and more women began their cinematographic career as directors of fiction films. The earlier tendency of women's filmmaking which had emerged in the early 1970s (and continued throughout the 1970s) was more concerned with activist documentaries on 'women's' issues such as abortion, rape and/or contraception. Coline Serreau followed both path-ways, starting with writing the script of her first fiction film (*Pourquoi pas!*, which she only made in 1977) and then making a documentary. After finishing Bertuccelli's film, she decided to make a film which would illustrate the *droit à la parole* (right to speak) of those who are usually deprived of it. She failed to obtain funding from the Centre National du Cinéma (CNC) and French television, and no producer wished to back her project either. Her multiple attempts to find financial support eventually paid off when she met Antoinette Fouque, 'head' of the women's publish-ing company Des Femmes (see below) who immediately agreed to give her 50,000 French francs without even signing a contract. Serreau spent it all on film material and began to interview women all over France, 'des femmes de tous les milieux sociaux, ouvrières, paysannes, bourgeoises, et de tous les âges'[4] (Serreau 1978b: 9). Her initial wish was to make a film about utopia. She declared that 'je voulais faire un film qui se serait appelé Utopie, dans lequel les femmes auraient décrit très concrètement la société qu'elles rêvaient'[5] (*ibid.*). Although none of the women in the interviews actually talked about utopia, all of them use the conditional or the hypothetical 'if' when speaking, therefore 're-creating', albeit mentally, their lives. Seven months later Serreau ended up with more than 24 hours of interviews and no money left. After months spent trying to finance the editing, she

---

4 'Women from all social classes, working class, agricultural workers, bourgeoises, and from all generations.'

5 'I wanted to make a film which would have been entitled Utopia, in which women would have described very precisely the society they dreamed of.'

managed with the help of friends and volunteers to reduce the 24 hours into a film of 90 minutes. At the same time, she applied for the *avance sur recettes* for her first fiction film *Pourquoi pas!*. This system, introduced by the CNC in 1959, lends money to debutant filmmakers after a committee examines their scripts and helps to explain the continuing annual input of new and young filmmakers in France. Although the amount allocated by the CNC does not cover the total expenses, it provides a much needed financial support for beginners. More recently, the system has ceased to apply only to beginners, and more experienced filmmakers can still apply after making their first feature film. Serreau has benefited from the new system from *Pourquoi pas!* onwards.

It was only after she was able to show extracts of her first documentary that Serreau finally received the coveted *avance*, after several earlier failures. She was awarded 600,000 French francs which allowed her to finish the editing of *Mais qu'est-ce qu'elles veulent?* The amount allocated by the CNC represented a little less than a quarter of the final cost of the film (2.5 million French francs). Among the other potential funding bodies was the French third television channel, the then FR3, whose managers changed their mind after learning about the homosexual element of the film. Although *Mais qu'est-ce qu'elles veulent?* was selected for the 1977 Cannes Festival (in May) in the section 'L'air du Temps', it was only distributed in Paris on 8 March 1978. The date was not chosen at random, as it has been International Women's Day since 1904. The film attracted immediate acclaim from critics across the whole political spectrum, from the mainstream as well as the specialist press, even from those who could not possibly be accused of being pro-feminist (with the particular exception of the far-right publication *Minute* which dismissed the film as boring in a few sentences). Coline Serreau was not unknown at the time since *Pourquoi pas!* had been released in France a few months earlier (21 December 1977) and had been awarded both the Georges Sadoul Prize and the prize of the women's magazine *Elle*.

Refusal of labels

The end of the 1970s can therefore be seen as a key moment in Serreau's career, as many hailed her as a major and promising filmmaker. Although she was also labelled a feminist director, she was unwilling to be reduced to such limited typing and often emphasised in the numerous interviews she gave at the time that she was not a 'professional feminist'. In an article devoted to women filmmakers as a recognition of the growing number of female directors and published in 1977, before *Pourquoi pas!*, she expressed her refusal of categorisation by denying the importance of her gender in her films: 'Je ne suis pas une femme qui fait du cinéma: je suis quelqu'un qui fait du cinéma'[6] (Gauteur 1977: 24). On the other hand, she recurrently stressed the importance of feminism alongside other key movements: 'Le marxisme, la psychanalyse et le féminisme sont au XXe siècle des instruments de lutte et de travail qui ont tout remis en question et dont on ne peut se passer'[7] (Serreau 1978d: 29). Later in 1978, she declared that: 'le mouvement des femmes ... on ne dira jamais assez ce qu'on lui doit, ce qu'on lui doit tous depuis 10 ans. Il change la face de cette société ... C'est un nouveau moyen d'investigation du monde'[8] (Serreau 1978a: 4).

Feminism was not the only label which Serreau refused. She did not want to be seen only as a 'serious' filmmaker either. She expressed her wish to make her audience think while at the same time entertaining them. She regularly underlined the fact that one can make films which talk about important and/or serious topics while at the same time amusing the audience, in the way that Bertolt Brecht used drama. Nor does she want to be seen as an *auteur* in the sense of sole artistic creator of the film. She denied the traditional divide between *auteur* and mainstream film which is – in her view – so typical of France: 'En France, on considère en

6 'I am not a woman who makes films, I am someone who makes films.'

7 'Marxism, psychoanalysis and feminism are in our century fighting and working tools which have questioned everything and which are indispensable.'

8 'No one can stress enough our debt to the women's movement for the last 10 years. It changes the society we live in ... It is a new means of analysing the world.'

général les films d'auteur comme des films automatiquement ennuyeux, et qui ne sont pas faits pour le grand public, et moi je refuse absolument et définitivement cette catégorisation là'[9] (Serreau 1978a: 1). Critical of the amateurism of the *Nouvelle Vague* and of some *auteur* films made in the 1970s, Coline Serreau stresses the importance of combining technical expertise with artistic vision in the filmmaking process, thus valorising the creative role of all members of the team from actors to technicians to director. Her refusal of hierarchies co-exists, however, with a pragmatic recognition that the director carries the responsibility of leadership. For example, despite her desire for equality in the making of *Qu'est-ce qu'on attend pour être heureux!* – which went as far as using the same font size for all the actors' names on the film poster – she was quite ready to justify placing her own name clearly at the top.

For Serreau there is a need to 'défétichiser le metteur-en-scène'[10] (Serreau 1982c: 43) by seeing the directorial role not only in terms of artistry but also in terms of a painstaking and highly skilled craft. Far from the makeshift tendency (*bricolage*) which in her view characterises some of her fellow filmmakers' work, she insists on extreme attention to detail and wants to be part of the filmmaking process from start to finish. She describes her behaviour on the set: 'il faut que je fourre mon nez partout. Je ne laisse à personne le soin de faire les cadres, je suis toujours présente au montage. D'artiste, je deviens artisane'[11] (Serreau 1978d: 27–9).

Her concern for meticulous detail extends to the actors as well. She is probably one of the few French film directors always to rehearse her script with the actors as if it were a play. Drawing from her theatrical experience, she greatly esteems the physical side of drama acting and often refers to the significance of the

9 'In France, people tend to automatically view *auteur* films as boring films which are not aimed at a mainstream audience. I absolutely and definitely refuse this sort of categorisation.'
10 'Defetichise the role of the director.'
11 'I have to poke my nose into everything. I never leave anyone in charge of setting the frames and I always attend the editing session. From being an artist, I become an artisan.'

body and the voice. To achieve or, more precisely, to make the actors achieve the maximum potential on the set, she sometimes devotes half of the overall filming time to rehearsals.[12] She explains her choice of technique by the idea that; 'on a beau avoir tout prévu, ne rien laisser au hasard, les acteurs enrichissent énormément les personnages et les situations'[13] (Serreau 1982c: 46).

This aspect of her work probably explains why there is no improvisation at all in her films, even if it might sometimes look as if there were. She wants the actors to learn their part and to deliver it 'à la virgule près' (Serreau 1978d: 27–9) (down to the last comma). Far from the improvised and interactive verbal excesses associated with the *café-théâtre* – which she practised herself in the early 1970s – Serreau builds her film script alone in order to offer a coherent narrative: 'je cherchais, seule, des gags qui rebond-issent, qui fassent corps avec l'histoire du film, ses personnages, son sens'[14] (Serreau 1982c: 42). Being an actress as well as a director, she knows the difficulty of working without a written script; 'I hate to work with directors who don't have a set text. It is hard enough giving a good performance without being called upon to write the dialogue and collaborate on the direction as well' (Overbey 1978: 88).

Serreau's reputation as a serious feminist documentary filmmaker was reinforced in 1979 by her contribution to a series produced by the Institut National de l'Audiovisuel (INA) and devoted to grandmothers. The aim of the programme was to give a voice to an often ignored generation, that of women in their sixties or seventies, who were invited to share their memories in front of the camera. Coline Serreau was not the only woman filmmaker to participate in the project as well-known directors such as Chantal Ackerman (who made *Dis-moi* about Jewish grandmothers who, like her own, were deported to concentration camps during the

12 For example, the acting team of *Qu'est-ce qu'on attend pour être heureux!* rehearsed 6 hours a day for 5 weeks (out of 10).

13 No matter how much everything is planned, and nothing left to chance, [with rehearsal] the actors bring a lot to the characters and the situations.'

14 'I was looking, by myself, for jokes which would bounce, which would be at one with the film's narrative, its characters and its meaning.'

Second World War), as well as male directors such as Jean Eustache (who made *Odette Robert*), took part in the enterprise. Serreau's film, *Grand-mères de l'Islam*, could be seen as an appendix to her first documentary. Here again, she was able to give a voice to a group of women who, because of their gender, their age and their ethnic origin were regularly ignored by the mainstream media. She chose to portray Zora and Kheira, two Algerian women living in the south of France. All the films were broadcast on the then first public channel Télévision Française 1 (TF1) during the summer of 1980. French television was also to broadcast *Mais qu'est-ce qu'elles veulent?* in 1982, during the 'International Week of Women'.

The 1980s: moving towards comedy and drama

During the 1980s, Coline Serreau's career moved towards fiction, and she worked both for the cinema and the theatre. The two strands of her career were never entirely separate but fed into each other; Serreau has never restricted herself to one genre or one art only. Similarly, her desire to entertain is always linked to a wish to reflect on more 'serious' matters. Her multiple artistic skills, especially her drama 'heritage', were already obvious in her first fiction film, through the casting of theatre actors. Thus Mario Gonzalez (Louis in *Pourquoi pas!*) often played with Ariane Mnouchkine and her Théâtre du Soleil,[15] and Christine Murillo (Alex in *Pourquoi pas!*) was trained at the Conservatoire. The concentration on a single setting – the *pavillon de banlieue* (a suburban house) where the trio lives – in *Pourquoi pas!* was another theatrical tendency which was even more visible in Serreau's second fiction film, *Qu'est-ce qu'on attend pour être heureux!*,[16] whose title was borrowed from a song by Ray Ventura

15 Interestingly enough Ariane Mnouchkine also made her film debut in the 1970s, starting in 1974 with *1789*, a film on the making and staging of her play about the French Revolution, and then in 1978 her unforgettable *Molière*.

16 The film, partly financed by the previously mentioned system of *avance sur recettes*, was part of the French selection at the film festival of Venice in 1982.

and in which, according to Serreau, 'tout se déroule dans un seul lieu, en un seul jour, une seule action, comme une tragédie classique'[17] (Serreau 1982a). The narrative centres on the shooting of an advert for a car for which Serreau gathered a troupe of artists, both as characters and real performers.[18] Her former *café-théâtre* partner at the Théâtre de Poche (Paris), Romain Bouteille (with whom she performed in his play *Le Soir des diplomates* in 1973), plays one of the leading parts. Alongside the musicians and trapeze artists already present in a few shots of *Pourquoi pas!* appear many other artists such as clowns (an interesting aspect as it has now become the term Serreau sometimes uses to talk about herself), tap and classical dancers, and opera singers. In other words, all forms of art are represented from the 'high brow' to the 'low brow' although this sort of hierarchy would be dismissed by Serreau herself as she declared that she wanted to show 'l'égalité absolue de tous les acteurs'[19] (Serreau 1982a). This desire for equal treatment for all is to be found not only in the size of the actors' names on the poster of the film but also in the amount of their wages. This aspect is part of the utopia or the 'desire for something else' reminiscent of the May '68 slogans which Serreau wanted to illustrate in her film through an optimistic perception that art and beauty can flourish among chaos. The film could therefore be seen as another version of the famous slogan 'sous les pavés la plage'.[20]

Although the film has often been compared with Fellini's *Prova di Orchestra* (Orchestra rehearsal) made in 1978 and which reveals a lot of similarities with Serreau's (though she had not seen the film at the time), the message is radically different from one rehearsal to the next. While the Italian director showed that

17 'Everything happens in a single place, in one day, with only one action, as in classical tragedy.'
18 The poster with the actors' team was quite similar to a music band very popular at the time, called *le Big Bazar* (the big mess) led by Michel Fugain. The band, inspired by May '68 brought together musicians as well as clowns, acrobats and singers.
19 'the absolute equality of all the actors'.
20 Which means literally, 'there is a beach beneath the asphalt'; and metaphorically; 'beneath the harsh reality lies a brighter tomorrow'.

chaos would lead to fascism, Serreau in her allegorical tale about society, human relationships and the role of artists within society demonstrates that there is still some hope, and that chaos too can be fruitful. She defined her film as 'un appel aux spectateurs de tous les âges et de toutes les conditions par le truchement du divertissement, à ne pas accepter l'inacceptable. Pas demain, maintenant. Les lendemains qui chantent, non. C'est aujourd'hui que ça devrait chanter.'[21] She also justified her choice by saying that: 'je choisis délibérément l'utopie heureuse, parce qu'il est impossible de donner une solution concrète, immédiate à de tels problèmes, qui mettent en fait en cause tout le fonctionnement de la société'.[22] After the release of *Pourquoi pas!*, Serreau had explained that her next project would be related to the 1789 French Revolution. It is interesting that the revolutions critics referred to in reviews of *Qu'est-ce qu'on attend!* were either the *printemps de Prague* (the Prague spring) or May '68.

Like the demonstrators and strikers of 1968, Serreau's group of artists react against the unreasonable demands of what they perceive to be an oppressive regime. Serreau shows (albeit entertainingly) that commercial imperatives lead to the artists being asked to perform artistic tasks for which they are not specifically trained. Thus the Fred Astaire and Ginger Rogers look-alike tap dancers must sing in the rain, the opera singers have to throw custard pies and the classical dancers to perform stunts. In scenes reminiscent of the silent era and strongly influenced by Mark Sennet's and Charlie Chaplin's films (the latter being a favourite of Serreau), she denounces the waste of artistic talents by producers whose only concern is money. The influence of Potter's *Hellzapoppin* (1941) is also very strong in this gigantic bustle which ends with the rebellion of the despised artists who, after trying all day long to accept their fate, spontaneously start their

21 'An appeal to the audience, whatever their age and social origin, through entertainment, not to accept the unacceptable. Not tomorrow but today. Brighter tomorrows? No thanks. Today should be brighter.'
22 'I deliberately choose happy utopia, because it is impossible to bring concrete and immediate solutions to such problems which in fact call into question the whole way society functions.'

own mini-revolution against those representing power and authority on the set.

Despite highly positive reviews (including from the far-right paper *Minute*), the film was a commercial failure. Was it, as has often been suggested, that the mood had changed and that the post-May 1981 euphoria engendered by the election of a socialist government had somehow watered down the desire and need for 'something different'? The widespread enthusiasm which followed the arrival of the first left-wing government since the Popular Front could explain the disaffection of the film's audience.[23] Indeed, for many in France, the 'lendemains qui chantent' had arrived and were there to stay, after the morose period which had followed May '68, and more especially the seven-year government of Valéry Giscard d'Estaing preceding Mitterrand's. It seemed, as far as Serreau was concerned, that the utopia and utopian mood she had so cherished during the previous decade, and which was a recurrent aspect of her previous films, was no longer the dominant mood. As will be seen next, this does not mean that she gave it up altogether. It would be fairer to say that she 'adapted' it to the 1980s in the two films she made during this decade.

A miraculous baby

This relative failure of a project which meant a lot to her might explain the gap between this film and her next one, made in 1985. Not that Serreau stopped working on new projects. Her next one after *Qu'est-ce qu'on attend pour être heureux!* was the writing–rewriting of an old script about a female Casanova entitled *Giova* (Lejeune 1987: 198). It was a silent film (as was *Chari-Bohu*, another script she wrote in 1990 and which was not accepted either by the CNC). After a few unsuccessful applications for funding, she started a new script whose tone and content were this time inspired by a mixture of some *café-théâtre* ingredients skilfully added to a 1980s' version of the *vaudeville*. She received

23 The coalition of the Fourth Republic (1945–56), although it included socialist ministers, was not led by a socialist prime minister.

the *avance sur recettes* from the CNC, but still encountered many difficulties in finding a producer. The reasons for the several initial rejections of the film that was to become *Trois hommes et un couffin* are many and varied. Her 'reputation' as a feminist filmmaker probably did not help her at a time when feminism was seen as dead – despite the socialist government's creation of a ministry for women. There was also a general reluctance among producers to distribute small-budget films (*Trois hommes et un couffin* cost only 9.7 million French francs). Comments were made as well about the choice of almost unknown actors. It is true to say that with the exception of André Dussolier – Jacques, the biological father of the baby in the film – who had previously played in *auteur* films with directors such as E. Rohmer, F. Truffaut, J. Rivette and A. Resnais while continuing a career on stage, the main actors were not well known to French audiences. The name of Roland Giraud (Michel) was associated with more popular films in which he had small parts. Michel Boujenah's career was mainly on stage where he exploited his Jewish *pied-noir* cultural heritage in one-man shows.[24] Both men came from the *café-théâtre* tradition, and it is ironic that the odd one out in the planned casting was Dussolier who initially did not fit, never having played comedy before. A further problem arose from the impossibility of neatly categorising the film. Serreau's films were generally considered as *auteur* cinema but here she had chosen to employ the genre of comedy, more usually associated with commercial cinema.

Trois hommes et un couffin was an overwhelming commercial and critical success. The film was top of the box-office list of 1985, ahead of *Rambo*. It was the sort of 'miracle' which rarely happens, given the initial problems of finding a producer and financing the film. The film was at first given only limited release in twenty-two cinemas in Paris, and that after a meagre advertising campaign. Yet publicity by word of mouth worked so well that three weeks later, with a rise of 69 per cent between the first and the third week's figures, a further eleven cinemas were showing the film,

24 'Pied-noir' is the name given to French people who lived in North Africa before the independence.

and it went on to become the phenomenon of the year. The film was awarded three *Césars* (the French Oscars) including best film and best script of the year, and was nominated for the American Oscar of the best foreign film. It is worth adding here that the *Césars* are rarely awarded to comedies or to the comedians acting in them. The only other occurrence is *Les Ripoux* (Zidi, 1984). As far as actors and actresses are concerned, they tend to receive a *César* only once they play in non-comic films, as was the case with the former *café-théâtre* comedians Coluche, Anémone and Michel Blanc.

Two months after the film's release, the producer Jean-François Lepetit, almost completely unknown before then, was approached by major American companies who wanted to buy the rights for an American remake. He finally sold them to the Walt Disney company and until the last minute Coline Serreau herself was to direct the remake. She went to the United States to rewrite the script in order to adapt it to the North American audience. An extract published in *Avant-Scène Cinéma* in January 1987 still presented Serreau as the director of the American version. A few months before the beginning of the shooting, she decided to give up the project after growing misunderstandings related to what 'rewriting' actually meant for both sides. According to Lepetit, 'pour eux [les Américains], c'est ou bon pour l'audience, ou pas bon pour l'audience. Pour un auteur comme Coline, c'est dur à avaler'[25] (Serreau 1987). An American male director then took over. Leonard Nimoy, a former *Star Trek* star (Spock), was chosen to direct the American version *Three Men and a Baby*, with another television star, Magnum, aka Tom Selleck, playing Peter (Pierre in the French version).[26]

Following her phenomenal success as a director, Coline Serreau decided to return to the stage, five years after her last stage performance. She explains her absence on stage by the lack of offers received which is – in her view – linked to a hierarchical French system: 'On a fini par considérer la mise en scène comme une ascension sociale: redevenir acteur, après cela serait en

25 'For them [the Americans], it is either good for the audience or bad for the audience. This is quite difficult for Coline as an *auteur* to swallow.'
26 More details are given on the remake in Chapter 3.

quelque sorte déchoir'[27] (Serreau 1986). Since the mid-1980s, she has resumed her acting career, and is now leading an 'artistic double-life', often shooting during the day and performing on stage in the evening. A few months after the release of *Trois hommes et un couffin*, she was playing Maman Lapin (Mummy Rabbit) in *Lapin Lapin* directed by Beno Besson. Written by Serreau under the pseudonym of Elie Bourquin,[28] the play was first staged in Paris in 1986 (Théâtre de la Ville) and then in Berlin in 1992 by Beno Besson and on tour in 1996 when it received a *Molière* (the French equivalent of the *Césars* for drama). The use of a pseudonym should not come as a surprise as she had previously declared: 'si je publiais ... ce ne serait pas sous mon nom'[29] (1978c: 13). However, her acting in a play that she had written looked promising since in the same article she had also said that: 'je n'ai jamais pu publier, comme le fait ma mère et je n'ai jamais pu écrire pour le théâtre, mettre en scène, comme le faisait mon père'[30] (*ibid.*). In 1998, she was directing and performing in *Le Salon d'été* (a play she wrote), to be performed in France later that year.

It is rather difficult to dissociate Serreau's films and plays as far as the content is concerned since her principal concerns and ideas recur in both. This is another aspect of her work which is detailed and analysed in the next chapter.

Since *Trois hommes et un couffin*, Coline Serreau has become a *valeur sûre* of French cinema, although none of her subsequent films (*Romuald et Juliette*, 1989; *La Crise*, 1992; and *La Belle Verte*, 1996) reproduced the 'miracle' of 1985. The success of *Trois hommes* had interesting consequences as all her films enjoyed a second 'career' on the small screen in Europe and beyond. Millions of European television viewers have watched *Romuald et Juliette* which is now a 'classic' film for European channels. With a

27 'Directing is seen as the top of the social scale: coming back on stage as an actor is therefore seen as a failure.'

28 A link was made between the pseudonym and the title of the first novel published in 1955 by Coline's mother, Geneviève Serreau, and entitled *Le Soldat Bourquin*.

29 'If I was to publish, I would not use my real name.'

30 'I have never been able to publish as my mother does, and I have never been able to write plays and direct them as my father did.'

screening on all the European television channels in 1996, the film has attracted more than 6 million viewers, including 4 million for the June–July period only. The screening on European television channels of *La Crise* since 1994 has also increased the viewing figures. The film was first released in France in 1992 and was awarded the *César* 1993 for the best script.

Rivals within the same camp? French cinema and television

Relations between cinema and television have historically been difficult, in France as elsewhere. Cinema has accused the younger medium (television in France only gained mass popularity in the late 1960s) of stealing its audience, and even of destroying the film industry. However, the relationship has changed dramatically since the mid-1980s, with a series of bills and reforms that have modified the links between big and small screen to such an extent that almost all the films made in France are directly or indirectly financed by French television. The bill passed under the first socialist government in 1986 introduced a compulsory system whereby all the channels whether public or private have to give 5 per cent of their annual turnover to help the financing of French cinema. Collaboration between television and cinema can also take different forms. Thus in 1991, Amnesty International asked thirty directors to make a very short – unpaid – film of 3 minutes in 35 millimetres to celebrate the organisation's thirtieth birthday. *Contre l'oubli* (*Against Forgetfulness*) was the title of the film, made up of the thirty shorts, which was released in Paris, Lyons and Strasbourg in December 1991. They had previously been broadcast individually on all the French channels between 10 November and 10 December,[31] with the notable exception of TF1, the first private channel which refused to show them. Coline Serreau's film was made with the French protest singer Jacques Higelin, who pleads for the release of two jurists jailed in Malawi.

Serreau has been involved in another similar project. In March

31 Each film was screened several times on one day only.

1997, she was approached by the association Handicap International to make a film denouncing the use of landmines. Ten directors from France and beyond (including for France, Bertrand Tavernier, Mathieu Kassovitz and Pierre Jolivet) were asked to make a short film (3 minutes).[32] The film *Lumières sur un massacre*, made up of the ten shorts, was broadcast on French channels in November and December 1997 before being released in French cinemas throughout France. Serreau's film, entitled *L'Enfant*, is set in the boardroom of a company specialising in landmines. The meeting is interrupted by the arrival of a child victim of these deadly weapons.

In the 1990s, Serreau has been touring with most of her stage productions, with texts of her own such as *Quisaitout et Grobêta*, which was awarded four *Molières* in 1994, *Le Théâtre de verdure* and *Lapin Lapin*. All plays were directed by Beno Besson, a director who met Coline Serreau's father Jean-Marie in 1942 before another crucial encounter with Bertolt Brecht in 1948 in Berlin.

Although mainly known nowadays for her films and plays, Coline Serreau did not initially train as a stage actress or a film director, a feature she shares not only with many of her female contemporaries but also with her predecessors. It is therefore worth outlining major aspects and figures of the rarely written history of women and the French cinema in relation to this element of Serreau's career.

Women and filmmaking in France

Women film directors in France have tended to '[come] to cinema via circuitous routes' (Hayward 1992: 19). This was the case for Alice Guy, the earliest French filmmaker who started her career as early as 1896 (that is, a year after cinema was invented); for Germaine Dulac, another famous director who made her first film in 1916; and later for Agnès Varda, the 'mother of the New Wave' whose first film was released in 1955 (Hayward 1992: 30).

32 Coline Serreau told me that none of the British and American directors contacted for the project were willing to participate.

The golden pathway to start a cinematographic career after the Second World War was the Institut des Hautes Etudes Cinématographiques (IDHEC; that is, the Higher Institute of Film Studies), later replaced by the Institut de Formation et Enseignement pour les Métiers de l'Image et du Son (FEMIS), the most famous cinema school where women were admitted (after taking a competitive entrance examination like all students-to-be) but were strongly advised not to specialise in film direction. Female students were therefore sent to more 'feminine' courses of studies, that is, editing, continuity girl, make-up or costumes. This is illustrated by the account of one female candidate: 'All the women who passed the entrance examination knew that they wouldn't be allowed into the film-directing course' (quoted by Forbes 1992: 83). It is worth adding here that women accounted for only 4 per cent of the students in 1974. The technical aspects of the cinema (sound, photography and camera) were considered 'masculine' ones and various arguments were given to discourage women from entering this male preserve including the weight of the material and the level of technology involved. This argument became less and less valid, especially after the New Wave film directors introduced new filming techniques, such as the extensive use of lighter – and cheaper – equipment (mainly the French camera *Eclair Cameflex* invented in 1948 but hardly used before the New Wave) needed for location shooting (as opposed to studio shooting). This led to a 'democratisation' of filmmaking which accounted for the greater access of women to roles behind the camera. Another way to train as a film director was to become the assistant of some famous male director. Here again, very few women were offered this kind of opportunity. Those who did often refer to the fact that they were usually the only women on the set save the continuity girl. Marie Epstein (born 1899), who started her cinematographic career in the 1920s as a scriptwriter, is in this regard an exception. She was the first to receive the Pathé Consortium cinema prize for *Les Mains qui meurent*. She worked as co-director with the director Levy, with an equal share of responsibilities (Lejeune 1987: 51).

It is worth noting that, until the late 1960s, the elements

mentioned above prevented the vast majority of women from directing films. The financial input required to start filming was a further deterrent for all but the most affluent women, which probably explains why women more often than not opted for short – and cheap – films. May '68 and the early 1970s radically changed the French cinematographic landscape as 'many professionally trained women entered film making at that point and released their first feature films. At the same time, a new generation of (often untrained) women directors made militant documentaries on issues such as abortion, work, motherhood' (Kuhn 1990: 165). In this regard, as in many others, May '68 was a trigger for women as well as for many other minorities to start making films.

The impact of May '68

May '68 is considered by historians as a watershed in French society as well as in French culture. According to Jacques Doniol-Valcroze writing in August 1968, 'the movement of May is irreversible' (quoted by Harvey 1978: 3). This sense of irreversibility was widespread. 'In the minds of those who took part ... nothing would ever be the same again. ... [May '68] was and remains a symbolic moment, a break in the history of contemporary France' (Forbes and Kelly 1995: 186). The so-called 'events' or 'revolution' began at the new university of Nanterre in the suburbs of Paris at the beginning of May. Though it started with student protests against the French higher education system, the Vietnam war, traditional left-wing political parties and sexual oppression within French society, the student movement rapidly became widespread and affected other sectors of French society. Following the brutal repression of students gathering in the Quartier Latin after some arrests were made, and more especially after what was to be called *La Nuit des Barricades* on 10 May, workers' unions joined the students' actions. In mid-May (13 May), a massive demonstration took place, involving students' unions as well as teachers' and workers'. From then on, the movement spread to the whole nation and many factories throughout the

country were occupied. Massive strikes and demonstrations para-
lysed the whole country, bringing the de Gaulle government to the
verge of collapse. By the end of May, 10 million were on strike in
several if not all areas of French society. A parallel was established
with the very strong social movements linked to the Popular Front
in 1936. As will be shown later, this is not the only point of
comparison with this specific period of French history. The media
and the arts were affected and involved as several examples
illustrate, from the cancellation of the Cannes Film Festival and
the declaration of the Etats Généraux du Cinéma on 17 May to the
massive strike at the government-controlled Office de Radio-
diffusion–Télévision Française (ORTF) during the last week of
May, the day after the meeting of the government with union
leaders on 24 May. After the Accords de Grenelle (Grenelle conference) as the meeting was called, the movement lost its strength
and appeal, as workers were not willing to compromise and accept
the deal offered by their unions' leaders. On 30 May, de Gaulle
declared the dissolution of the General Assembly and called for a
general election. By the beginning of June, things were almost
back to normal and it seemed in some areas as if nothing had
really happened. The Gaullists won the general election in 1969,
though de Gaulle resigned as president the same year.

Even if the 'revolution' eventually failed, its impact was still
very strong at the beginning of the 1970s. 'A cultural revolution
had taken place. For a visitor to France before and after May '68
the change was almost tangible' (Forbes and Kelly 1995: 185). This
does not mean, however, that society radically changed immediately
after May '68. From a political point of view, the 1970s mark the
end of Gaullism and the beginning of a new era in French political
life. Georges Pompidou, then de Gaulle's prime minister took
over as president in 1969 after de Gaulle's resignation. He
remained in power until his death in 1974. These five years are
often seen as years of 'calm, torpor and gloom' as the effects of the
euphoric period of May '68 seemed to fade away. However, these
same years also saw the reconstruction of the Left around the
programme commun (common programme) between the Parti
Communiste Français (PCF) and the Parti Socialiste (PS) in 1972,

a multiplicity of political and financial scandals, and the emergence of something different in French society. Women's roles and representations – and desire to change them – were some of the most obvious and visible aspects of this transformation.

Women in France in the 1970s: women's movements and the sexual revolution

As mentioned above, despite the fact that May '68 was the generator of many of the social and political movements which took place in the 1970s, there were a few years where it seemed that nothing had really changed. As far as women's actions, and actions in favour of women, were concerned, there was a gap after the Neuwirth law passed in 1967 which authorised contraception. Despite a few important moments in the early 1970s, such as the creation of the Mouvement de Libération des Femmes (MLF) and the manifesto in favour of abortion signed by 343 well-known women,[33] it was only in 1974 that action was taken at government level. The *secrétariat d'Etat à la condition féminine* (secretary of state to women's condition) was put in place by the right-wing government of Valéry Giscard d'Estaing in 1974 and held by the former journalist Françoise Giroud. The same year and following massive demonstrations by women's groups, the *Loi Veil* (named after the then female minister of health) legalising abortion was presented to the National Assembly on 11 November and promulgated after the vote on 17 January 1975. Despite the vote, French women had to wait until 1979 for the right to abort to be actually put into practice (the final bill was passed on 30 November 1979). From 1982, abortion was paid for by the Sécurité Sociale (Social Security). The year 1975 was declared *l'année de la femme* (the Year of Women) in France.

In the couple of years which immediately followed May '68 the French cinema was not very different from before May '68, unlike the mid-1970s (especially after 1973–74), which could be summarised

33 More details of this law and other laws related to women's rights and sexuality are given in the last chapter.

by one of the May '68 slogans, 'soyez réalistes, demandez l'impossible' (be realistic, ask for the impossible). As far as women were concerned, the demands were abundant and varied. The means of expressing them were extremely varied as well. The right to speak (*droit à la parole*) advocated by all the minorities (silenced and silent) before May '68 was exercised on an extremely large scale after May '68, from amateurish newspapers to more professional ones, from makeshift publications to organised publishing companies, from action groups' videos to individual full-length feature films. There was a profusion of collectives, action groups, communities of all kinds willing to 'speak out'. Despite internal rivalries and tensions, what emerged from innumerable productions of the time was the feeling of being on the verge of something new, something waiting to be created, and that all the actors, known or unknown, of this massive change within French society were willing to produce. The will to rethink and transform existing institutions expanded inevitably to cinema, and particularly to women's role within the industry: 'le cinéma, de tous les modes d'expression, est celui qui a le plus réagi aux mutations des vingt cinq dernières années'[34] (Audé 1981: 219). In the past twenty-five years, women's movements have claimed their right to self-determination which the women's lib's slogan 'notre corps nous appartient' (our body belongs to us) shows. They have tried to change their status as sexual objects during a decade when objectification was rife in cinema particularly in the form of the porn industry.[35]

Pornography and French cinema

The 1970s in France were the golden age of the French pornographic industry. Although initially labelled 'erotic' cinema, French porn was soon to be called 'porn' and the 'infamous' letter X was soon to mark all the films belonging to this category. Before the

34 'cinema is the means of expression which has the most reacted to the changes of the last 25 years'.

35 More details of women's struggles regarding sexuality are developed in Chapter 5.

1970s, nudity (of female bodies of course) was scarce and very much fought against. After the scandal of Vadim's film *Et Dieu créa la femme* (*And God Created Woman*) two decades earlier (1956) in which Brigitte Bardot's naked body could be glimpsed in the very first scenes, any attempt to show bare flesh was banned. A strict control was exercised from 1958 by the then Commission de Contrôle. Many examples, such as the scandal created by Malle's *Les Amants* in 1958, the initial banning of Godard's *La Femme mariée*, the battle against censorship after Rivette's *La Religieuse* was banned in 1966, illustrate the strong opposition in France (as elsewhere) to the visual representation of sexuality. The release in 1971 of Louis Malle's film *Le Souffle au cœur*, which dealt with incest between a mother and her youngest son, or of Bertolucci's controversial *Last Tango in Paris* in 1972 were seen as the signs that attitudes were changing.

It was, however, the release of the adaptation of the erotic best-seller *Emmanuelle* in June 1974 which blurred the thin boundaries between eroticism and pornography. Distributed in a commercial cinema as an erotic movie, the film allowed porn to gain some 'respectability'. It ran for a few months on the Champs Elysées, the same avenue on which a porn cinema opened in September 1974. A year after *Emmanuelle*, the first 'hard core' film (that is, showing explicit sex) was distributed in nine cinemas in Paris, both mainstream and art houses. The concern expressed by the then secretary of state at the Ministry of Culture, Michel Guy, led to the law nicknamed *la loi X*, passed in October 1975 by the right-wing majority of the National Assembly under the government of Valéry Giscard d'Estaing. The law did not ban porn as such. It was aimed at reducing the import of foreign porn films, at preventing the 'visibility' of porn films and porn cinemas, in other words at putting porn on the sidelines. Different devices were used: heavy taxation on imports, a ban on showing visual posters of the film – which led to an increase in sexually explicit titles, and the labelling of all porn films as X-rated. Although this did not immediately and completely stop porn films being made in the 1970s (as an example, 51 films out of the 118 French films released between August 1977 and February 1978 were classified X), the law eventually put an end to the success of porn in the cinema. By the early 1980s, the joint effects of the screening of porn films on French television, together with the increase in VCRs destroyed what remained of a once flourishing industry.

Women and French cinema in the 1970s

Among the silent and silenced minorities of the earlier decades (or centuries), women were by and large the biggest group. It is worth adding here, although this is not specifically the aim nor the subject of this book, that another minority group which started speaking out at the same time was the community of immigrants. Interestingly enough, many common points can be found between the two groups.

In October 1973 a group of French women sharing a similar interest in cinema created an association called Musidora. The name was not chosen at random and was very symbolic. Musidora was 'one of the silent cinema's greatest stars' (Vincendeau 1995: 300). Born Jeanne Roques in 1889, she started her acting career before the First World War. She became famous with Louis Feuillade's celebrated series *Les Vampires* (1915–16) in which she played the character of Irma Vep (an anagram of vampire). After her first failed try as a film director (a cinematographic adaptation of the writer Colette's *L'Ingénue libertine*) in 1916, she directed in 1917 her first film, *La Vagabonde* by Colette, in which she played the leading part. In order to gain independence *vis-à-vis* the Italian producer of the film, she created her own production company La Société des Films Musidora. From then on, she produced all her own films (seven in total, six of which were made between 1917 and 1922 in France as well as in Spain). Her artistic talents were wide-ranging: she was a writer as well as a painter, dancer and musician. She was not only 'France's first vamp' but was also 'crowned "queen of the cinema" in 1926' (Vincendeau 1995: 300). Her numerous talents and her pioneering experience as a woman filmmaker explain the choice of her name by her indirect heirs sixteen years after her death.

According to the creators of the non-profit association Musidora, its aims were to promote the creation and the distribution of video and cinema products made by women; to follow up researches on cinematographic representations and roles of women in both male and female films; to organise meetings in order to improve the distribution and reception of women's films. One of the major actions of Musidora was the creation of the first ever international women (only) film festival in France. The first event organised with the help of the CNC took place in Paris in 1974. In 1976, the newly born women's publishing company Editions des Femmes, published a book of testimony by the women of Musidora, *Paroles ... elles tournent.* Coline Serreau did publish – under a pseudonym – two texts in the book, the aim of which, according to the editors, was to give any women interested the right and the space to do so. 'Carte blanche avait été donnée à toute femme, spécialiste ou non de cinéma qui désirait en *parler* [their emphasis]. Aucun texte n'a été refusé'[36] (Musidora 1976: 5). Interestingly enough, this publishing company was created in 1974 by the feminist Antoinette Fouque, from the group Psychanalyse et Politique, as a limited company. It was a collective project typical of the mood of the time, directed by women, for women and where, according to Fouque, 'Aucune n'est patron ou chef de service, ou directrice de collection'[37] (Picq 1993: 211). The group Des Femmes opened its first bookshop in Paris in 1974, a second in Marseille in 1976, and a third in Lyons in 1977. Although Des Femmes' 1979 appropriation of the MLF acronym as their registered trademark was to split the French women's movement and antagonise the majority of feminists, their publishing projects of the mid-1970s provided an important space in which women could be seen and heard – not least women filmmakers.

36 'Any woman, either specialist of cinema or not who wished to *talk* about it, was given a free hand. Not a single text was rejected.'
37 'No one is the boss or the manager, or the series editor.'

Women's film festivals

Musidora, later criticised for its 'feminist terrorism' (quoted by
Audé 1981: 96), constituted a major breakthrough for and by
women. It gave women filmmakers the first opportunity to get
and to work together. Following the first short-lived association
(which organised a second women (only) film festival in Paris in
1975), other groups emerged such as Femmes/médias and Ciné-
Femmes-International. The Festival International de Films de
Femmes (FIFF) was created in 1979 and took place initially in the
Paris suburb of Sceaux. Its organisers and creators acknowledge
the filiation between their festival and Musidora's, even if they
recognise as well that they work with different criteria (mixing of
gender during the screenings of the films in competition). At the
second festival, they also wanted to illustrate what they saw as 'un
deuxième temps de la prise de parole des femmes dans le cinéma
... Depuis les années 75–76, les femmes commencent à faire de la
fiction, c'est-à-dire à libérer leurs fantasmes'[38] (Gémeaux 1980:
71). The FIFF was later to move to another neighbouring town of
the department, Créteil, where it continues to attract tens of
thousands of spectators of both sexes (35,000 in 1989). Serreau's
Qu'est-ce qu'on attend pour être heureux! was screened at Créteil,
together with *Trois hommes et un couffin*. It was during the same
festival (1986), with the presence of Coline Serreau and Agnès
Varda (who was presenting her film *Sans toit ni loi*), that the
dilemma between *auteur* and commercial cinema was discussed.
It is worth noting here that despite the recurrent presence of
French women directors at Créteil – as part of a special section on
French women filmmakers (in 1986 and 1987) not competing, or
as guests attending the première of their films (such as Agnès
Varda in 1988 with *Jane B by Agnès V*, or Coline Serreau in 1989
with *Romuald et Juliette*) – there is a general reluctance among
French women filmmakers to have their films entered in the
competition itself, and the rule according to which the films have

38 'A second phase in the speaking out of women in the cinema ... Since the years
   1975–76, women have started to make fiction films, in other words, to release
   their fantasies.'

to be shown for the first time does not justify this. This unwilling-
ness to participate fully in a festival dedicated to women's films
can be explained mainly by the general refusal of French women
directors to be defined in terms of gender. Despite the general
climate of the late 1970s, and in particular the widespread
emphasis on gender and sexual identities and the importance of
the women's movement in all aspects of French society, French
female directors resisted at a very early stage a classification based
on gender. Contradictory as it may seem, this is a major specificity
of French feminism. According to Ginette Vincendeau, 'that
women's cinema cannot be equated with feminism is now a
commonplace, but it is perhaps in France that the separation is
most obvious' (1987: 11). Notwithstanding the fact that French
feminist writers (with key figures and key texts such as, among
others, Simone de Beauvoir's *Le Deuxième Sexe* (*The Second Sex*,
1948), Luce Irigaray's *Spéculum de l'autre femme* (1974) or *Ce sexe
qui n'en est pas un* (1977)) inspired most of the early feminist
movements in France and later feminist film theories in the
Anglo-Saxon world, French female directors dissociated themselves from a gendered vision of society. For Vincendeau, the
current position of French women filmmakers could be described
as falling between two stools. On the one hand, 'they lack a
credible ideological framework in terms of group allegiance, on
the other, they still hold only marginal positions in the industry'
(Vincendeau 1987: 9). She also emphasises the fact that 'the
connection between theoretical debates about gender and feminism and women's film-making in France is at best oblique and at
worst conflictual, as there is virtually no indigenous feminist film
theory or theorizing of gender and sexual difference in relation to
the cinema, and precious little awareness of these issues in French
film criticism' (Vincendeau 1987: 5). Could that be another 'side-
effect' of the universalist republican tradition of French society
inherited from the Enlightenment and the French Revolution and
according to which no distinction should be made between French
people whatever their gender, class and/or religion? Whatever the
answer, as early as 1978 directors such as Coline Serreau (who,
however, recognised elsewhere the importance of feminism

which in her view was as important as Marxism) and Diane Kurys declared their refusal of their films being labelled 'women's films'.[39]

Women's films from the 1970s onwards

Things have changed a lot for female filmmakers in France since the late 1970s and early 1980s. After the 'first wave' in the 1970s followed a second one in the mid- and late 1980s. Women directors now account for around 20 per cent of the total of filmmakers in France, a situation which is unique in the world. This does not mean, however, that the new generation of female directors who started their career in the mid-1980s feels concerned and/or interested by the idea of 'gender', and they seem to follow their elders as far as their attendance at women's film festivals is concerned. After the generation of the 'baby boomer' filmmakers came a generation born mostly in the mid- and late 1960s, who grew up in the 1970s and whose main concern was not necessarily women's rights. Despite (or because of?) efforts made by the first socialist government to bring changes to the situation of women in many areas, feminism was considered dead in the early 1980s. For some, the creation of a ministry for women in 1981 meant that women's issues were taken care of at governmental level. The Ministry for Women, led by minister Yvette Roudy (1981–86), modified existing legislation by introducing a new set of laws to augment women's autonomy, to legally guarantee their equality with men and to fight sexism in the workplace and in the media. The budget devoted to the ministry increased from 92 million (French francs) in 1982 to 129 million in 1986. In the meantime, most publishing companies and periodicals born in the aftermath of May '68 collapsed. Some feminist publishers justified their disappearance by saying that '"cultural" feminism is not dead: it simply no longer speaks, it has

---

39 When using this expression, one has to keep in mind that its meaning is quite different from the 'women's films' originating from the USA. When we use it, we mean 'films made by women'.

no name because it has entered people's heads, including women's ... The fact that feminist journals disappear one by one is therefore natural: they have reached their objectives' (quoted by Vincendeau 1987: 4). While French feminist theoreticians were widely read in the Anglo-Saxon world, and while their texts became the cornerstone of feminist film theory/ies, they were almost forgotten in France.

France in the 1980s and 1990s

In the 1980s France was becoming increasingly concerned with other issues and other 'minorities' whose voice was not as strong as the women's groups' during the previous decade. Feminism and women's rights were seen as old-fashioned and *passé*. The explosion of violence in the French suburbs (*la crise des banlieues*), which started during the summer of 1981, revealed to a majority of French people the consequences of the economic crisis and the extent of social exclusion. A decade before the *fracture sociale* (social fracture) became a fashionable political term (surprisingly coined by the right-wing gaullist party of Jacques Chirac during the 1995 general elections), a new expression was used to describe those who had lost all social benefits. The emergence of the *nouveaux pauvres* (new poor) led in 1988 (11 October) to the creation of the Revenu Minimum d'Insertion (RMI: the minimum benefit for those with no other source of income) by the socialist government led by the prime minister Michel Rocard.

Immigration became a political issue in France where a second generation of North African immigrants was emerging and fighting a growing racism. The year 1983 was a very dark year for those who were from then on called *les beurs*.[40] After several clashes with the police in various towns in France (and particularly in the Lyons area), with tragic consequences and multiple killings of young Arabs by isolated individuals or racist gangs, a 'march for

40 The word 'beur' was coined by the second generation of North African immigrants and is a backward reading of Arab. It is still widely used to describe them.

equality' involving around forty North African youngsters from underprivileged areas took place from Lyons to Paris between October and December 1983. In 1984 a support group called France Plus was created by the youngsters to defend their rights, while another group initiated by the Socialist Party joined the struggle to fight racism. SOS Racisme appeared in December 1984. During the 1984 European elections, the score of the far-right party the Front National (National Front) led by Jean-Marie Le Pen (10.95 per cent) created a shock since the far right had never attracted so many voters. Exploiting the fear of insecurity and with a strong anti-immigration agenda, the Front National was to increase its score from one election to the next. Although Serreau does not explicitly refer to these aspects of French society in the 1980s and 1990s, her films do reflect some of the changes of these decades, for Serreau's cinema can in many ways be seen as political cinema.

References

Audé, F. (1981), *Ciné-modèle, cinéma d'elles*, Lausanne, L'Age d'Homme.

Avant-Scène Cinéma, '*Trois hommes et un couffin*', no. 356, January 1987. The whole issue is devoted to the film with complete film script, interview, stills and review articles.

Chevallier, J. (1983), 'En France: révoltes tous azimuths pour vivre autrement', in '1960–1980: vingt ans d'utopie au cinéma', *CinémAction*, no. 25, pp. 31–42.

Forbes, J. (1992), *The Cinema in France: After the New Wave*, London, British Film Institute/Macmillan.

Forbes, J. and M. Kelly (eds) (1995), *French Cultural Studies*, Oxford, Oxford University Press.

Gauteur, C. (1977), 'Elles ont tourné tout l'été', *Le Film Français*, no. 1689, 9 September, pp. 24–8.

Gémeaux (1980), '2ème festival de films de femmes à Sceaux', *Des Femmes en Mouvement*, March, pp. 71–2.

Harvey, S. (1978), *May 68 and Film Culture*, London, British Film Institute.

Hayward, S. (1992), 'A history of French cinema: 1895–1991: pioneering filmmakers (Guy, Dulac, Varda) and their heritage', *Paragraph*, 15: 1, pp. 19–37.

Hayward, S. (1993), *French National Cinema*, London, Routledge.

Hayward, S. (1996), *Key Concepts in Cinema Studies*, London, Routledge.

Jeancolas, J.-P. (1979), *Le Cinéma des Français: la Ve République*, Paris, Stock/Cinéma.

Kuhn, A. (1990), *The Women's Companion to International Film*, London, Virago.

Lejeune, P. (1987), *Le Cinéma des femmes*, Paris, Lherminier.

Musidora (des femmes de), (1976), *Paroles ... elles tournent*, Paris, Editions des Femmes.

Overbey, D. (1978), 'France: the Newest Wave', *Sight and Sound*, Spring, pp. 87–8.

Picq, F. (1993), *Libération des femmes: les années-mouvement*, Paris, Seuil.

Rémy, M. (1990), *De l'utopie à l'intégration: histoire des mouvements des femmes*, Paris, L'Harmattan.

Serreau, C. (1978a), 'Coline Serreau: la force des convictions et le plaisir du spectacle', interview in *Jeune Cinéma*, no. 110, April–May, pp. 1–7.

Serreau, C. (1978b), 'Coline Serreau: à propos de son film: *Mais qu'est-ce qu'elles veulent?*', interview in *Des Femmes en Mouvement*, February, pp. 9–10.

Serreau, C. (1978c), 'Planer ... Coline au trapèze', interview in *Des Femmes en Mouvement*, February, pp. 12–13.

Serreau, C. (1978d), 'Coline Serreau: une contestataire tranquille', interview in *La Revue du Cinéma: Image et Son*, no. 325, February, pp. 27–9.

Serreau, C. (1982a), 'Tentative de déclaration d'intentions', press copy of *Qu'est-ce qu'on attend pour être heureux!*.

Serreau, C. (1982b), 'Entretien avec Coline Serreau', interview in *Cinématographe*, July, pp. 21–3.

Serreau, C. (1982c), 'Coline Serreau: propos d'auteur', interview in *Cinéma 82*, no. 286, October, pp. 40–8.

Serreau, C. (1986), 'L'autre versant de la Coline', interview in *Le Nouvel Observateur*, 10 January.

Serreau, C. (1987), 'Trois hommes et Lepetit', interview in *Libération*, 22 December.

Serreau, C. (1993), *Quisaitout et Grobêta*, Paris, Actes Sud Papiers.

Vincendeau G. (ed.) (1986), 'Women as auteur-e-s: notes from Créteil', *Screen*, 27: 3–4, pp. 156–62.

Vincendeau, G. (1987), 'Women's cinema, film theory and feminism in France', *Screen*, 28: 4, pp. 4–18.

Vincendeau, G. (1988), 'Créteil 1988: ten years on', *Screen*, 29: 4, pp. 128–32.

Vincendeau, G. (1995), *Encyclopedia of European Cinema*, London, British Film Institute.

Zimmer, C. (1974), *Cinéma et politique*, Paris, Seghers.

2

A rebel with causes: Coline Serreau and politics (1972–96)

Coline Serreau's work on stage and on big or small screens was (and still is) strongly influenced by the political mood which succeeded May '68 in France. Her debut was clearly motivated by the sense of deep changes French women felt at the time. Although she did not actually join any of the various women's groups and movements, the films she made in the 1970s reflect most of their concerns. From the 1970s onwards, she has remained faithful to her initial beliefs, even if the changes within French society in the past twenty years are also evident in her own evolution as a filmmaker and dramatist. Like many other directors, she has chosen different ways of expressing this desire for 'something different' to be found in the 'political', 'militant' or 'activist' films which flourished in the 1970s. Her singularity lies not so much in the genres she opted for, but in her very personal way of exploiting them to create an original work.

This chapter will consider the specificity of French cinema in the 1970s before analysing in more detail Serreau's first film. Indeed, her documentary *Mais qu'est-ce qu'elles veulent?* may be seen as the director's manifesto and as a major contribution to women's struggle.

French cinema in the 1970s

French cinema after May '68 was increasingly becoming more political, more 'social' and realistic, but in quite a different way from the 'poetic realism' of the 1930s. According to A. Kuhn, 'May '68 may not have brought the "revolution in and through the cinema"; it nevertheless heralded a shift in both auteur and popular films towards a more socially conscious cinema' (Kuhn 1990: 163). The first moves towards a more 'liberated' cinema should not be exaggerated here, as censorship in the cinema was still very much in practice, either for political or for moral reasons. Thus, Charles Belmont and Marie Issartel's film about abortion (*Histoires d'A*, 1973) was banned for a year in France after its release in 1973. At about the same time, director Yves Boisset was not allowed to shoot some sequences of his film *L'Attentat* (1972), about the Algerian war, in a Paris airport and had to go to Geneva instead.

The second half of the 1970s, from the election of Valéry Giscard d'Estaing in 1974 until the victory of the socialists in May 1981, was influenced by the 'liberalism' of its president. Thus, the 'Veil Law' (*Loi Veil*) legalising abortion was passed in 1974, and as regards the cinema, the newly elected president made a declaration regarding censorship. A few days after his election, Giscard declared: 'Les libertés publiques sont et seront minutieusement respectées: plus d'écoutes, plus de censure, ni sur les films ni dans les prisons'[1] (Jeancolas 1979: 44). Although this declaration was not always applied, it was a step forward. This 'liberalism' explains the emergence of different films and topics. Or, to put it differently, French society became more visible in French cinema. If we use the distinction between 'subversion' and 'integration' when talking about the films of the time, it can be said that both 'subversive' and 'integrated' films tended to show a French society much more contemporary than before. What Jeancolas calls the 'vague contemporary', which for him characterises French cinema before the 1970s, became much more precise afterwards. The 'contemporary' was mostly expressed through socio-political films.

---

1 'Public liberties are and will be carefully respected: no more phone-tapping, no more censorship, neither in films nor in prisons.'

Socio-political films

It might be useful first to try to define what is meant by socio-
political films. For Christian Zimmer (who is representative of
certain left positions on cinema in the early 1970s), 'il y a politique
partout où il y a un rapport autorité-obéissance'² (Zimmer 1974:
7). The fact that this relation was widely visible in the 1960s, and
more so in and after 1968, does not prove for sure that 'political
cinema' appeared only in the 1960s. In his book *Cinéma et
politique*, Zimmer considers that from the very beginning there
were political films – among which he mentions *L'Affaire Dreyfus*
by Méliès and Pathé as early as 1899 – whose aim was, a few years
after the 'Dreyfus affair', to prove the innocence of the wrongly
accused Jewish officer. It can be added here that the film was
banned until 1950, which demonstrates, if that is necessary, that
film censorship in France started almost simultaneously with
cinema! In May 1936, the arrival of the Popular Front, the left-
wing government (a coalition comprising representatives of
several left-wing political parties) initially led by the socialist Léon
Blum, not only introduced several major social reforms (in areas
such as health and work), but also had a significant cultural
agenda. What became known as the 'Popular Front cinema' was
indeed a film movement which was aimed at propagating left-
wing ideas. Renoir's *La Vie est à nous* (1936) was financed by a
collective and was a manifesto for the French Communist Party.
The cinema was not the only field explored by the Popular Front
which contributed to many cultural experiments during its brief
access to political power (May 1936–October 1938).

The main difference, however, between 1970s' cinema and
that of the Popular Front is the fact that unlike the latter, the
former was the expression of a reaction against a right-wing
government, albeit 'liberal'. Many film directors of the time, male
and female, chose to make 'left-wing' fiction films as the *Cahiers
du Cinéma* labelled them. What the category meant was the deep
will to bring a change within the film industry through films

2 'there is politics everywhere where there is a relation between authority and
  obedience'.

which refused the alienation inherent to the commercial process of cultural production. Zimmer sees political films as 'un courant qui échappe à l'idéologie dominante' (1974: 10) (a current that escapes from the dominant ideology). He identifies several degrees of political films, from the most radical documentary to what he calls 'progressive films' which for him are 'tout ce qui peut augmenter notre connaissance du réel' (*ibid*.: 39) (the ones that can increase our knowledge of reality), but he insists that all political films should reject the technical perfection and the notion of success that for him are the aim of official ideology. The makers of political films were faced with two alternatives: filming different things in the same way or filming the same thing differently. For Zimmer and for the collaborators of the special issue of *Cinéma 70* on the topic, films should not exist just to tell stories, because there is never neutrality in the choice either of the stories or of the way they are told. In their view, any film expresses – by its very existence – ideological choices. Moreover, even if a film draws on 'real' events, it is not necessarily realistic, and the same argument is valid the other way round: realism (or in other words, the perfect visual imitation/representation of reality) does not necessarily imply reality. A quarrel around the concepts of 'real' and 'realism' led to opposition between *Les Cahiers du Cinéma* and *Cinéthique*, both of Marxist persuasion in 1970. The debate (triggered by Costa Gavras' political though mainstream films *Z* and *L'Aveu* released respectively in 1969 and 1970) centred on the possibility or otherwise of combining popular appeal with political effectiveness. The main contradiction is that for a political film to have an impact, to generate reactions and to change the dominant ideology, it has to be screened and viewed. In other words, to be seen it has to be distributed and is therefore in a way 'appropriated' by the very same dominant ideology. Some films, however, managed to surpass this apparent contradiction and the distinction between militant cinema and commercial cinema faded slightly when some militant films gained a wider audience than others (for example, there were 200,000 spectators for *Histoires d'A* although the film was officially banned).

Coline Serreau was very much aware of the dilemma which she

defined in 1978 in these terms: 'ceux qui cherchent à exprimer cette avant-garde ont tendance à cracher sur les moyens d'expression bourgeois'[3] (Serreau 1978c: 27). She herself disagreed with this position. In her view, there is a possibility of using mainstream culture to express things differently: 'Ce que je veux ... c'est m'approprier les possibilités, les moyens de cette culture, mais pour exprimer ce qui bouge. Je rejette complètement ce que celle-ci véhicule, mais dans le même temps, je sais bien que c'est de ce côté qu'il y a le "savoir faire"'[4] (*ibid.*). Using mainstream cinema (and cinematographic genre) to communicate more 'radical' ideas and to lead her audience to think differently is typical of Serreau's work, as mentioned in Chapter 1. It is also one of the main features of the *conte philosophique* (philosophical tale) as will be shown later.

We have defined the radical director's project as one of filming different things in the same way or filming the same thing differently. It is obvious when watching some 1970s' films that both alternatives are used by filmmakers to show the 'contemporary' mentioned earlier. It can be added here that socio-political films, without necessarily being political in the sense Zimmer gave, illustrate a post-1968 tendency that Michel de Certeau called *prise de parole* (literally, to take the right to speak), and that *prise de parole* gave a voice to those who had not previously gained access to speech, such as the working class, the ethnic minority and last but not least women. This 'speaking out' was obvious as well, albeit differently, in the 'utopian' film which coexisted with the socio-political film and was also strongly influenced by May '68. This is a major aspect of Serreau's work as shown later in this chapter.

3 'those who try to represent this avant-garde trend, tend to reject the bourgeois means of expression'.

4 'What I want ... is to take for myself the possibilities, the means this culture [mainstream] offers, but in order to express a different one, one which progresses. I totally reject what it conveys but in the meantime, I know that this is where the "know how" can be found.'

Utopia

Etymologically, the word 'utopia' derives from the Greek 'ou' (not) 'topos' (place), and thus means 'what has no place'. Since Thomas More's 1561 book entitled *Utopia*, the word has come to mean an imagined society that has (at least as yet) no place in reality. In France, the utopian tradition in literature is particularly marked in the period preceding and following the 1789 Revolution. It includes, for example, the eighteenth-century pre-Revolutionary texts of Voltaire and Diderot, and nineteenth-century models for harmonious communities such as the *Icarie* invented by Cabet (1788–1856), and the *phalanstère* of Fourier (1772–1837). Soon after the minor revolution of May 1968 came another utopia imagined by the feminist writer Christiane Rochefort in *Archaos ou le jardin étincelant* (Archaos or the sparkling garden, 1972). Across Europe, the twentieth century has also seen a strong tendency towards counter-utopias, or dystopias, for example in the literary texts of Aldous Huxley (*Brave New World*, 1932) and George Orwell (*1984*, 1949), and Fritz Lang's first counter-utopia in the history of cinema (*Metropolis*, 1927).

In the context of 1960s/1970s French cinema, utopianism can be seen not only in film texts, but also in the way filmmaking itself is perceived. The Etats Généraux du Cinéma (States General of Cinema 68 a clear reference to the 1789 French Revolution), presented the declarations of the rights of cinema (36 items). The introduction stated that 'Toute libération du cinéma, toute création de structures nouvelles doit commencer par une destruction des anciennes'[5] (quoted by Chevallier 1983: 31). As far as the content of the films is concerned, most of them illustrated one slogan from May '68: 'take our desires for reality'. For Guy Hennebelle, 'tout paraissait possible, en effet, dans les années soixante et plus encore peut-être dans les années soixante-dix'[6] (1983: 5).

Coline Serreau illustrated a specific type of utopia. According

5 'Any liberation of the cinema, any creation of new structures must start with the destruction of the old ones.'

6 'everything seemed possible in the 1960s and probably even more in the 1970s'.

to Daniel Serceau in his analysis of utopian films made in the 1970s, three directions were available for fiction film directors in their reinvention of realism: 'réalisme critique', 'utopique' or 'dialectique'. We shall concentrate here mainly on the second which he defines as the brand of realism to be found in film-makers who, 'donnant plus ou moins libre cours à leur imagin-ation, réalisent leur désir dans la représentation. Leur film anticipe la venue d'un monde qui reste à faire. La "révolution" paraît achevée dans la fiction, à défaut de l'être dans le monde objectif'[7] (Serceau 1983: 123). Although the association of 'realism' and 'utopian' might seem strikingly contradictory as what is meant is the initial presentation of the Ideal as reality. Thus, in *Pourquoi pas!*, the audience is immediately confronted with the *ménage à trois* without the threesome being an issue at all. The problems are elsewhere and certainly not in the unconventional relationship between the two men and the woman. Their 'family' or 'couple' is presented so naturally that it creates an almost automatic acceptance from the viewers. Far from criticising the existing norms of sexual behaviour, Serreau avoids this altogether by giving the trio all the appearances of the 'norm'. Far from making her characters eccentrics or outsiders, she legitimates their way of life by showing their obvious happiness and the total harmony they live in, a harmony only troubled by the traditional 'norm': Alex's ex-husband, Fernand's ex-wife and Louis' parents. (The film's content is discussed in more detail in Chapter 4).

However it was not only in fictional form that Serreau attempted to 'anticipate the arrival of a world ... still ... to be created'. The documentary – particularly in the post-1968 period also allowed the expression of a utopian will to imagine the world differently, and we have seen that Serreau's first attempt at directing – like that of many of her contemporaries – was within the documentary genre. Fiction was not always the most favoured medium for a new director, not only for ideological but also for

7 'giving more or less free rein to their imagination, realise their desire through representation. Their films anticipate the arrival of a world which, however, still has to be created. The "revolution" seems to be achieved in fiction, for want of being so in the objective world.'

financial reasons. Unlike fiction films, which usually imply a heavy technical and financial investment, documentaries could be made with a relatively small budget.

Documentaries

Despite a long tradition of non-fiction films in French cinema, documentaries are often ignored or underrated in festivals and cinema books alike. Although the period when Coline Serreau made her first documentary (*Mais qu'est-ce qu'elles veulent?*) is sometimes seen as a 'historical interlude', the quality of this first exercise in film direction has stood the test of time. A key moment in her career, the film is also important in the history of the French documentary overall and of women's activist films in particular. From the conditions of production to the content via the latent ideology it implies, the film epitomises the desire to 'film different things differently', typical of the 1970s. Before analysing the film in more detail, a brief reminder of the position of the documentary before and after the 'revolution' is needed to assess the specificity of Serreau's contribution to the genre.

'Le documentaire, à quoi ça sert?' (What are documentaries made for?)

It often happens in France that early documentaries are discovered only once their directors have become famous through their fiction films. This seems to imply a hierarchy within French cinema whereby the documentary would be half-way between the full-length feature film and the short fiction film, or even at the bottom of the league, if René Prédal's comment is to be believed: 'le documentaire est méprisé non seulement par rapport à la fiction de long métrage, mais aussi à l'intérieur même de l'univers du court métrage'[8] (1987a: 16). Shorts and documentaries are

8 'documentaries are despised, not only in relation to long-length fiction films, but also within the field of short films'.

more often than not the *parent pauvre* (poor relation) of the relatively wealthy long fiction film. This dichotomy was materialised in the old cinema programmes, when short documentaries (both words were/are often synonymous) were shown during the first part before the fiction films. Although several attempts have been made to help the financing of documentaries since the 1970s, they still account only for a minority of the overall number of films distributed in France which are allocated subsidies from the state. Despite the growing participation of the French television channels in the financial sponsoring of documentaries since the early 1980s, the genre seems to suffer from a general lack of interest from producers, distributors and the public, and a widespread misconception of its aims and objectives, which is summarised by the provocative question opening this paragraph (*CinémAction* 1987: 2).

The historical heritage of the genre comes from the naturalistic tradition: documentaries from the early days of the moving image were associated on the one hand with education and on the other hand with mere recording of reality. In France, the introduction of pedagogical films in teaching came as early as the inter-war period. While many at the time were concerned by the apparently anarchical development of the *théâtre de foire*, as fiction films were sometimes dubbed, the documentary was often seen as photography was then, that is as a scientific instrument. Despite the desire expressed by many ever since the early years of the twentieth century to get rid of this 'malédiction naturaliste des origines' (Gauthier 1987: 30) (the naturalistic malediction of its origins), the documentary is still associated with learning and therefore lacks the appeal of traditionally escapist fiction films. Traditional documentaries were seen – and often still are – as reproducing reality, not reinventing it, despite the fact that many directors from the 1950s onwards have often mixed fiction and non-fiction material in their films.

The definition of documentary varies according to different authors. The Georges Pompidou Centre in Paris, which has been organising a festival of documentaries, Cinéma du Réel, for the past twenty years and where around 2,000 documentaries are available to the public (including Serreau's *Mais qu'est-ce qu'elles veulent?*), defines it as: 'tout film ne requérant pas l'intervention de comédiens professionnels' (Prédal 1987b: 46) (any film which does not require professional actors). The Larousse dictionary of films defines it as: 'toute œuvre cinématographique, ne relevant pas de la fiction, qui s'attache à décrire ou à resituer le réel'[9] (Passek 1995: 635). The stark opposition between fiction and reality oversimplifies the relationship between the genres, and a combination of both definitions seems more suitable for our purpose.

Renewal of the genre? French documentaries in the 1950s

An aspect to consider when talking about the French documentary is the fact that it was considered as an exercise for apprentice filmmakers. Over the last forty years, directors have often learnt their job by directing short documentaries before moving on to fiction films. For some directors, this was a way of avoiding the long training of an assistantship. Another argument in favour of the short as training was a financial one. The only available state funding before the creation of the *avance sur recettes* (1959) was the *prime à la qualité* put in place in 1954 by the CNC for documentaries and shorts (Forbes 1992: 14). Shorts were sometimes also commissioned by individuals or institutions. Whereas the conditions of production considerably influenced the content of the documentary, some filmmakers did succeed in subverting the restricted framework they were initially assigned.

Although most of the novice filmmakers subsequently made fiction films, some documentary directors were (and still are) nothing but documentary directors and have never been tempted to move to fiction films. Thus, directors like Chris Marker and Raymond Depardon have been making documentaries in France for 45 years and 30 years respectively and are hailed as major directors in their field. Others have happily mixed fiction and

9 'any cinematographic work which does not belong to fiction and whose aim is to describe or re-create reality'.

documentary films throughout their career. Agnès Varda is one of the rare directors – unlike Alain Resnais who started with documentaries in the 1950s with the acclaimed *Guernica* (1950) and *Nuit et Brouillard* (1956) and is now devoting his time to fiction film only – who continues to make documentaries as well as fiction films.

As seen in Chapter 1, May '68 is one of the key moments of twentieth-century French political, social and cultural history. In the French cinema, the 'events' led to a social and political awareness reminiscent of the Popular Front cinema in the 1930s. The documentary is the genre which, maybe more than others, did benefit from the changes. This does not mean, however, that documentaries were apolitical or asocial before 1968. On the contrary, the influence of the New Wave was already present in documentaries made by directors such as Alain Resnais, Chris Marker and Agnès Varda, to name some of the most famous. They brought another dimension to the genre by trying to renew it. Some modified the existing classic editing system, while others innovated by transforming the relationship between sound and images. Instead of the neutral comment in voice-over of the traditional documentary, which often repeated what the images had already shown, directors such as Marker, Varda or Resnais brought their own gaze and perspective to their films. The equation whereby documentary equals objectivity was no longer valid as 'le respect du réel propre au documentaire n'empêche pas les cinéastes d'imposer leur regard par la rigueur d'une mise en scène qui s'approprie en quelque sorte l'espace et le temps d'un monde peuplé de personnages aux marges de la fiction'[10] (Prédal 1987c: 76). From the 1950s onwards, the directors in question not only revised the definition and the creation of the documentary, but they also questioned the existing boundaries which surrounded the genre: boundaries between fiction and documentary, between the representation of reality and the indirect criticism of what the

10 'the respect for reality, peculiar to the documentary, does not prevent directors imposing their own viewpoint through rigorous directing which adopts in some ways the space and time of a world inhabited by characters on the margins of fiction'.

images showed, and between the *auteur* touch they brought to their films even when they made commissioned films, and the accepted idea that 'les images parlent d'elles-mêmes' (images speak for themselves). They announced in many ways what was soon to be called the 'cinéma direct' in the mid-1950s and 1960s.

Cinéma direct, cinéma-vérité: new techniques, new visions

The *cinéma direct* was first influenced by the British Free Cinema in the mid-1950s. Far from illustrating or informing on events or general topics as classic documentaries did, the *cinéma direct* was more concerned with human beings, not just as representing humanity as a whole, but as specific individuals as well. The methods used were not, however, those of traditional interviews (typical of television reports) with the interviewer in control of the questions and the shot/countershot system (interviewer/inter-viewee) which meant a perfect match between sound and images. In France from the late 1950s onwards, French film directors discovered the attempts by Quebec film directors Pierre Perrault and Michel Brault to renew the genre of the documentary. During the summer of 1960, the French sociologist Edgar Morin and the ethnographer/director Jean Rouch made *Chronique d'un été*, in which using light and portable material (such as the camera Coutant and the tape recorder Nagra) they ask Parisians: 'êtes-vous heureux?' (are you happy?). Morin and Rouch called their experience *nouveau cinéma-vérité*, from *Kinopravda* (Cinetruth) the pioneering work of the Russian Dziga Vertov (1896–1954). Chris Marker used similar techniques when making his documentary *Le Joli Mai* in 1963.

The introduction of new techniques, such as the Eclair 16 camera which by 1965 was no longer connected to the sound recorder, allowed a new conception of the link sound–image. For some, this technical achievement was as important as the creation of cinema itself (Serceau 1987a: 85). It played a major role in the following decade.

New brand/new trends: militant activist documentary (1968–81)

Although – as briefly seen in Chapter 1 – some political and social films were made before May '68, the *entre-deux-mai* period was the golden age of the genre.[11] As early as 17 May 1968, the Etats Généraux du Cinéma expressed the will of the authors to 'réaliser une rupture idéologique avec le cinéma bourgeois'[12] and to opt for 'l'utilisation du film comme arme politique'[13] (quoted by Ballérini 1987: 91). Thanks to the technical progress mentioned above, directors could go almost anywhere with their camera and film what had previously been either ignored or hidden. French cinema, with the notable exception of filmmakers like René Vautier who reported about the 'events' in Algeria between 1954 and 1962 at the time they happened, had regularly disregarded some recent major political and/or historical moments. The Algerian war played a key role in the development of activist cinema. A minority of filmmakers tried, as early as 1955 for Vautier and the team who made *Une Nation, l'Algérie*, to break a silence that censorship alone can not entirely explain. May '68 provided the perfect opportunity to carry on the struggle. Many directors throughout the 1970s put into practice the statements made during the Etats Généraux du Cinéma whose manifesto 'Pour un cinéma militant' defines how films can and must become weapons: 'Il peut donner des informations que la presse bourgeoise écrite et parlée ignore délibérément ...; il peut aider à analyser les mécanismes du système capitaliste afin d'en révéler les contradictions et par là aider à les combattre; il peut servir à populariser, à comprendre, à tirer des enseignements de toutes les formes de lutte révolution-naire, remplissant dans tous ces cas une fonction critique et moralisatrice'[14] (quoted by Hennebelle 1976: 31).

---

11 The term literally means 'inter-May' and refers to the period between May '68 and May 1981, date of the socialist victory at the general elections. It was initially coined by the historian Pascal Ory.

12 'to bring about an ideological break with bourgeois cinemas'.

13 'the use of film as a political weapon'.

14 'It can give information that bourgeois papers and radios deliberately ignore; it can help to analyse the mechanisms of the capitalist system in order to reveal its contradictions and thereby serve to fight it; it can be used to popularise, to

Although the group who started the Etats Généraux du Cinéma was short-lived and disappeared by the 1970s, the many and varied action groups which emerged at the beginning of the decade took over. The enormous commercial success of *Z* – the 'fiction' film by activist director Costa-Gavras (1970) released in mainstream cinemas throughout France which dealt with the dictatorship of the so-called colonels in Greece – showed expectations for 'something different' which many activists, known or unknown, novices or experienced, were willing to live up to. Be they regional, political, rural, immigrant or feminist, these collectives used documentaries to set and express their own political agendas. With unequal success and technical resources (16mm film, Super 8 or video), they produced thousands of films to denounce, testify or castigate. We shall concentrate now in more detail on women's documentaries.

Women's documentaries in the 1970s

As suggested in the first chapter, women probably represented the biggest group of the silenced 'minorities'. It is therefore the one which, maybe more than others, did take the opportunity in the 1970s to make itself heard loud and clear. Cinema and video, together with more traditional tools such as publishing, provided women and their action groups with another 'weapon'. For the women-only organisation Videa created in July 1974, for example, women had to create their own images, of themselves as well as of others. They justify their decision to establish their action group by saying that: 'on ne voit pas pourquoi la vidéo échapperait à l'idéologie patriarcale véhiculée par les autres médias. Les femmes se heurtent encore à une mise à l'écart, à un rôle de muses ou de collaboratrices subalternes, bénévoles et reconnaissantes'[15] (VIDEA

---

understand and to draw lessons from all forms of revolutionary struggle, therefore fulfilling a critical and moralising purpose.'

15 'we don't see why video would not be affected by the patriarchal ideology spread by the other medias. Women still have to face rejection, have to perform the role of muses, or of subordinate, volunteer and grateful collaborators.'

1976: 147). Although it is impossible to assess precisely the impact of one film on the society in which it was produced, it is true to say that films such as *Histoires d'A*, made in 1973 by Charles Belmont and Marie Issartel, played a key role in the general debate surrounding abortion at the time. Alongside Serreau's documentary, *Histoires d'A* remains in the militant and feminist archives as a key date and moment.

Unlike many women filmmakers who made documentaries in the 1970s, Serreau did not belong to any action group and her film is in many ways very individual, in the conception as well as in the making. Travelling throughout France for six months to meet women who had heard about her project and were willing to speak out, Serreau took only one technician with her. As well as the financial reason for working with a small team, she also wanted to establish a different relationship with the speakers where 'les règles d'or étaient: discrétion, écoute maximale, ne pas presser les gens, respecter leurs silences, ne pas savoir à l'avance ce qu'on veut qu'ils disent, ne jamais les interrompre'[16] (Serreau 1978b: 9). In this respect, Serreau's respect for her interviewees distinguishes her from many of her contemporaries.

Polyphony of desires and regrets: *Mais qu'est-ce qu'elles veulent?*

Mais qu'est-ce qu'elles veulent? was once described as '*Le Chagrin et la pitié* des femmes' (de Gaspéri 1978) (a female *Sorrow and the Pity*). The comparison is not totally innocent. Ophuls' film made in 1970 and released in France in 1971 represents a determining moment in the history of French cinema and documentary as well as in the history of French people and their troubled relationship with the painful memories of the Second World War. Banned from television until 1981, Ophuls' four-hour-long film was distributed in cinemas in France and was extremely successful, especially when one keeps in mind the general reluctance of the

16 'the golden rules were: to be discrete, to be ready to listen as much as possible, not to be pushy, to respect their silences, not to prejudge what we want them to say and never to interrupt them'.

audience *vis-à-vis* documentaries. A historical document made of a mixture of interviews and period newsreels, it was not an activist film (*film militant*) as such, if one recalls the definition of the *cinéma militant* suggested by Guy Hennebelle that: 'c'est un cinéma qui ... est le plus souvent tourné en marge du système ... est presque toujours produit avec des petits moyens ..., se met d'emblée, et par définition au service de la classe ouvrière'[17] (1976: 11). Its aims were, however, to demystify the official version of France's recent history.

Although it cannot be said that the people who were interviewed in Ophuls' film had previously been deprived of the 'right to speak' (on the contrary, some of the interviewees did not always seem too willing to express themselves), the most important element of comparison is that all the testimonies from one documentary to the other spelt out clearly and sometimes loudly what many knew but did not want to acknowledge, that is, in the case of Serreau's film, that many women in France were still oppressed, alienated and often deprived of some basic rights. Moreover, their desire for change was obvious to the viewers.

The eight women who talk individually about their personal lives, their disappointments, their alienation and their frustrations, offer a polyphony of their gender's 'écrabouillement économique et idéologique' (their being economically and ideologically crushed), to quote Coline Serreau (1978d), and express what many French women could easily identify with at the time (and some probably still do). One could almost say that this makes these women stand as allegories of women's position/s in French society. From one region to the next, from one class and one generation to the other, they create a sort of mosaic of French womanhood. They are ordinary women who talk about their mundane daily lives, their history and their regrets, very often aware that things might, should or could be different. Most of them express a willingness for change, while only one seems convinced – even if she sounds as if she were trying to convince herself – that women should accept their lot which is to have and raise children. Be they farmers,

17 'it is a cinema which ... is often made on the margins ... which is almost always produced with very little means ... and which stands straightaway and by definition on the side of the working class'.

working class, middle class, porn actress, anorexic, caretaker or retired pastor, they all illustrate a form of oppression and repression, either economic, sexual, physical or religious. Some can name and identify it while others would probably be surprised if told that their claims are the same as the MLF's. None is a self-confessed feminist which was something Serreau wanted, some of them do not even seem to know that women's groups exist. And yet their testimonies show that they are all mentally ready for a change.

Coline Serreau insisted in many interviews on the subjectivity that editing implies. Let us remember that there were initially twenty-four hours of film from which only 6 per cent was kept. In choosing to keep certain testimonies but not others, Serreau decides on the perspective she wants to give her film, exercising the legitimate power all directors have to show certain things and not others. In this case, it is not as if she were dissimulating key evidence or silencing witnesses. There is little doubt that a large majority of the women interviewed during the six months Serreau spent shooting her film reported similar statements whatever their age and the class they belonged to, and wherever they came from. Without going as far as talking of a manipulation of/by the images,[18] it is true to say that the film is constructed as an argument and the order of appearance of the interviewees in the film is not chosen at random. The guiding principle from one woman to the next is their varied experience of 'enslavement'. As extreme as the word may sound, it refers to their recurrent use of terms such as *esclaves* (slaves), *bagne* (jail) and *tyrannie* (tyranny). Moreover, within each interview, the director selected what was the most relevant in the woman's speech for her illustration of her alienation. This also applies to the other participants. The managing director of the factory where some of the speakers work did try to prevent the distribution of the film on the basis that he felt his comments had been misinterpreted.

Similar comments could be made about the distribution of time allocated to each speaker. The working-class women take the lion's share with around 40 per cent of the total film (which

18 Let us not forget that *any* film relies on editing, which is manipulation, if only etymologically.

should not come as much of a surprise considering on the one hand the social context of the time and on the other Serreau's comments about her commitment to and belief in Marxism), while other categories appear only briefly. The shortest sequence is the middle-class housewife. Although the time assigned to the participants can affect audience reception, it is difficult to assess whether there was a conscious decision by the director to offer a 'hierarchy' between more and less deserving causes. It would be too easy, as Daniel Serceau did, to dismiss the film as sheer manipulation on the basis that the choice of shots differs from one group to the next and that this is in itself a proof of favouritism (1987b: 88–105).

However, even if the film is built as a political statement, it differs from the more typical activist films by the attention devoted by Serreau to the quality of the images. Ideology does not, in her view, necessarily prevent aestheticism nor visual pleasure. She regrets the lack of finish of many militant films and stresses the importance of the visual aspect of her documentary. She underlines her desire to make something stimulating and to avoid the boredom usually associated with documentaries: 'Je me sens responsable vis-à-vis du public, je n'ai pas le droit de l'ennuyer'[19] (Serreau 1978b: 9).

Talking about the editing, she declared that: 'C'est comme ça que je m'exprime dans le film, je n'y interviens jamais autrement. C'est le spectacle. A travers le spectacle, je remets en question un modèle de société, par le sensible et par l'intellect. J'ai voulu soigner particulièrement les images. J'ai mis les images que j'aime ... la partie visuelle est très importante'[20] (Serreau 1977). She never interferes nor intervenes in the interview and is neither seen nor heard. A male voice puts questions to the two male speakers (the managing director and the porn filmmaker) in what looks like a more traditional face-to-face. The situation is different with the main female speakers and rare are the cases where the

19 'I feel responsible *vis-à-vis* my audience and I have no right to bore them.'
20 'This is the way I express myself in the film, the only way I intervene. It is spectacle. Through spectacle I question a model of society not only intellectually but also at the level of feelings. I wanted to pay particular attention to the images. I chose images I like ... The visual side of the film is very important.'

interviewees actually speak to the camera. Her extensive use of voice-over allows the images, chosen by Serreau, not necessarily to repeat or illustrate the content of the 'monologue', but on the contrary to contradict, oppose and sometimes indirectly criticise it. There is no neutrality in what is shown, be it women's demonstrations, political posters, pictures related to the topic in question or visual descriptions of the speakers' conditions of life.

Between each sequence, the same shot is shown as a symbolic leitmotiv illustrating the change to come. By choosing the recurrent image of the sea and growing waves, Serreau wanted to represent water as a force which could or would bring fluctuations: 'l'eau, c'est ce qui est dans nos veines, dans nos ventres, qui dort et qui parfois se réveille, et c'est la tempête'[21] (Serreau 1978b: 9).

Southern farmers

The film starts with the testimonies of two female farmers in the South of France. After shots of the restricted domestic setting of a rural kitchen follow close-ups of female faces of different generations. The following sequence shows wider shots of a sunny countryside whose beauty is reinforced by musical extracts from a J. S. Bach organ work. A woman then starts talking in voice-over while the camera presents images of nature before displaying the speaker. She sets the tone of the entire film by referring to the harsh life in the countryside: 'pour une femme, c'était le bagne' (for a woman it was like hard labour). Born in a farmer's family and married to a farmer, she regrets her lack of education before justifying it by saying: 'C'était comme ça' (that's how it was). The second woman comes from a rural background and has always hated the countryside. She seems very bitter when talking about her life and her failed marriage. She is very critical of the unfair system which condemns women to economic dependency while men are independent. She is very much aware of the extent of women's alienation: 'Les gosses dépendent du père ... Tout est

21 'water is what runs in our veins, in our wombs, what is asleep and sometimes wakes up, and then it becomes a storm'.

pour les hommes ... les femmes n'ont pas de droits ... Allez donc refaire les lois, les femmes seront toujours des esclaves! ... J'ai le cafard.'[22] She never talks directly to the camera but is always standing back, away from the action, from her children, which clearly reinforces her lack of integration in her adopted milieu.

Northern working-class women

The sequences which follow take place in the north of France where several working-class women employed at a local clothing factory tell of their lives. Different regions, different accents, different living conditions but similar alienation. This extract is the longest lasting for almost forty minutes. Unlike the previous women, these gained financial 'autonomy' as they are wage-earners. However, their fate does not look any better. They describe the inhuman conditions of work, the exploitation and the humiliation they endure from their – male – superiors, from the head of their workshop to the manager. The account of their daily effort, their never-ending struggle to be treated as human beings in a factory they have dubbed 'l'abattoir' (the slaughterhouse), is interrupted by comments by the managing director. Far from listening or even understanding their grievances (such as not being entitled to drink, or not having showers available), he speaks in a caricatural way about production, productivity and profits while criticising his female employees. The contrast between his speech and his employees' is striking. The whole extract could be seen as a visual guide to capitalism for beginners. More than the other testimonies, this one illustrates Serreau's concern in this film to show the relationship between class and gender, and between Marxism and feminism. Unlike the farmers, the working-class women rarely refer to their personal life. Their main focus is the power relationships they encounter at work as workers more than as women. Their speech is highly political and they are

22 'Kids depend on their father ... Men get everything ... women have no rights ... What's the point of changing the laws, women will always be slaves! ... I feel depressed.'

presented as active union members. Several shots of demonstrations show them carrying banners and marching with their fellow workers. They often refer to the need of women to be united.

Le Charme discret de la bourgeoisie[23]

The managing director's conservative view that 'il faut bien un chef dans la famille' (families need a [male] leader) and his comparison that in this regard the factory is like a family are echoed in the following sequence by a middle-class woman whose opening words are the positive (and, for her, obviously reassuring) statement that: 'la femme est le complément de l'homme, jamais son égale' (women are a complement to men, never their equal). A Catholic housewife whose husband is managing director of a local factory,[24] she voices the concern of women of her class regarding the changing situation of women in society. Strongly attached to patriarchal traditions, she unwillingly and unconsciously illustrates another form of alienation. Her testimony is an inventory of *clichés* and stereotypes typical of her class, from the fear of the masculinisation of women and the consequent feminisation of men, to her objection to abortion (unless for very specific and limited cases). As in the previous extract, the editing allows some interesting contrasts. Her account in voice-over is juxtaposed with a series of different images which often seem to offer an alternative to her speech – a fixed shot of the daily right-wing newspaper *Le Figaro* reporting on the Veil Law and illegal abortion, a succession of close-ups of the factory workers and their boss, and wider shots of a women's demonstration whose banners claim: 'Instinct maternel. Pouvoir paternel' (Maternal instinct. Paternal power). This seems to reinforce the view that, on the one hand she is on the employer's side, and on the other that she represents her class and not her sex group. For what she expresses is almost always an

---

23 Buñuel's film (1972) is a satire of the bourgeoisie and denounces its hypocrisy, selfishness and cynicism hidden behind its good manners.

24 Some critics see her as the wife of the manager previously heard, which is actually not obvious or certain.

echo of men's perception of women, especially regarding women's main role as mother. At the same time, despite her claim that the MLF makes her laugh, she expresses an awareness of the unfairness of the housewife's condition by stating that it is not really seen as a job, that it is not paid and that it is often boring. Like the others, she declares her regrets: 'Si on m'en avait laissé l'occasion, je crois que j'aurais été une passionnée' (If I had been given the opportunity, I think I would have been passionate). The tone of her voice and the sadness of her face contradict her statement that she is a joyful woman. Although she is probably better off than the other interviewees, she still has a lot to object to even if she never directly criticises the system and lacks the perspective to realise the extent of her oppression. The fact that she takes part in the film is, however, very interesting as Serreau's criterion for choosing the interviewees was their desire to talk: 'le principe du tournage était que toutes les femmes qui avaient envie de parler seraient filmées' (the basic premise of the shooting was that all the women who wanted to talk would be filmed) (Serreau 1978b: 9). Her need and/or desire to be interviewed probably says a lot about her situation as it could be assumed that she wishes to 'speak out' as well. Her testimony is therefore quite ambiguous as she often tends to contradict herself. As the only representative of the 'Catholic–middle-class–housewife', her account is, however, crucial.

From repression to 'emancipation': the so-called 'femme libérée'

The next sequence starts with a shot of two women naked in a bath. The female voice-over is rapidly identified as belonging to one of the women, both porn actresses. Far from the uptight previous interviewee, the speaker seems at ease with her body and her nakedness despite the presence of the men surrounding her. A former student, the articulate and educated young woman explains how she got interested in pornography. She initially saw it as: 'une façon différente de vivre son corps' (a different way to accept one's body), but is now totally disillusioned. After seeing herself in her first film as a so-called 'femme libérée' (an emancipated woman), not only did she fail to recognise herself, but she sensed that she had been duped. A strong believer in women's sexual liberation, she felt dominated and oppressed by the very system she thought could emancipate her.

As with the working-class women and their manager, her testimony is interrupted by accounts from the porn film director Alberto. His perspective differs radically from hers, as his main reason for becoming a 'pornographer' is 'pour donner une image plus réelle de l'homme' (to give a more real image of men). While she talks of 'rapports de force', 'violation de la personnalité' and 'contraintes esthétiques' (power relationships, violation of personality, aesthetic coercions), the camera shows Alberto directing the two women in the bath. Then follow close-ups of very explicit pornographic material displaying sexual acts which offer a sharp contrast with Alberto's comment, when asked what he thinks about the MLF, that he is in favour of women's liberation. However, he rejects the idea of a sex/gender war and prefers to talk about 'des mouvements d'amitié entre les sexes' (friendship between sexes). The final statement is the actress's bitter confession that: 'Ça a été très dur pour moi d'assumer cette image que j'ai vue, comme ça, sur l'écran, d'un moi-même vu à travers les yeux d'Alberto ... C'était horrible ... et c'est ce sentiment d'échec qui est terrible, quoi, et qui m'oppresse complètement.'[25] Without knowing it, she echoes the claims made by other women, actresses or not, who decided to start making films in order to offer an alternative to the male gaze, since, as one put it, 'le regard des femmes, on ne le connaît pas' (Forrester 1976: 12) (women's gaze is not known).

From a body wrongly seen as a source of emancipation, the next sequence shows the tyranny it can lead to. The connection is made through the early comment by the actress that aesthetic criteria vary a lot depending on whether they are applied to a man or a woman.

25 'It was very hard for me to accept this image I watched on the screen, of a me seen through Alberto's eyes ... It was dreadful ... and this feeling of failure is appalling and depresses me a lot.'

'Fat is a feminist issue'

The woman we shall refer to as the anorexic starts by saying that she finds herself ugly. She expresses her obsession with her weight and how it is an 'alienation fantastique' (extreme alienation) as this 'obligation d'être mince' (obligation to be thin) is, in her view, worse than all the others because '[elle est] intérieure, n'est pas dite et ne se voit pas' ([it is] inside, unsaid and unseen). She also talks about sexuality and expresses her dislike of the idea that traditional heterosexual relationships necessarily imply penetration. She regrets the fact that it is the 'fin inéluctable' (inevitable ending) of sex.

Very lucid and extremely articulate, she explains how female bodies are put on display only when they are young and smooth. Using the cinema as an example, she denounces the unequal treatment of ageing stars. What is valorised and praised for one sex is rejected and denied for the other. A succession of pictures shows Charles Bronson in close-ups, followed by old women, one previously seen at the beginning of the film and the other who will be identified as the next speaker. French female stars follow them (Danielle Darrieux and Simone Signoret among others). Here again, the speaker reflects another claim made by female directors and summarised by Nicole Lise Bernheim: 'Une femme vieille devient sujet, en étant niée dans son sexe par les hommes et par elle-même ... Une vieille femme est asexuée, plus qu'un homme vieux ... Elle n'est plus rien, débris, n'étant même plus objet de désir, objet de film'[26] (1976: 39). From the stars she then moves on to talk about the situation in real life, when 'tu vois tous ces bonhommes, ils sont ridés, ravagés, qui ont trente six mentons, et qui sont tous avec des bonnes femmes très lisses'.[27]

26 'An old woman becomes subject, since her sexuality does not exist for men or for herself ... An old woman is more asexual than a man ... She is nothing, an old wreck, as she is no longer an object of desire, nor an object for a film.'
27 'you see all these old men, with wrinkles and thirty-six double chins, completely wrecked, who are all with very smooth women'.

God moves in mysterious ways

Far from the obsessive scrutiny of her body, the next interviewee is very much concerned by spiritual matters. A Swiss Protestant woman in her seventies, she is a former pastor and doctor in theology. As a mystical and religious person, she is highly disappointed by the way the Protestant Church treats women. As a pastor she could not marry and her initial idea was to spend eleven months in her parish and then stay the remaining one with her lover. When she got married, she lost her job. A mother of seven, she explains how her job was a way for her to say that 'la femme n'est pas qu'un utérus' (Women are not just a uterus). Her conclusion is that 'on dit que la religion et la maternité sont les deux choses qui matent une femme. Je ne suis pas matée'.[28]

Despite her regrets about being forced out of her parish, she is extremely quiet and composed, and especially when compared with the previous speaker. This does not prevent her from being highly critical of religious institutions in particular and of the patriarchal structure of society in general. She is one of the rare speakers to use language in a humorous way, indulging in puns and plays on words. Her tone is often ironical and she smiles a lot when explaining her ordeals. She declares that 'les femmes ne sont ni potiches, ni des bonniches mais des potières' (women are neither puppets, nor servants. They are potters – the pun is lost in translation) before declaring that 'la femme veut faire le ménage de l'Etat et enfanter des lois' (Women want to do the cleaning of the state and give birth to laws). Although this does not appear in her testimony, the ex-pastor has created an MLF group entitled Les Sorcières (The Witches). This could explain the fact that she is more lucid, aware and 'enlightened' than any of the others. At seventy, she is full of hope and believes that at last she will be able to do what she wants. She concludes by saying that: 'j'aime ce que j'ai fait mais je n'ai pas fait ce que j'aimais ... mais je vais le faire' (I like what I did but I have not done what I like ... but I am going to). This constructive optimism is also what characterises the last speaker.

28 'it is often said that religion and motherhood are the two things which tame women. I am not tamed'.

La veuve joyeuse (The merry widow)

After the firm assertion by the former pastor that despite her age her life is in front of her, this testimony offers a sort of echo that there is no age limit for women to be set free. This is even more interesting when, at the beginning of the interview, the narrator recalls what she initially thought of (wrongly) as being freedom: 'Le mariage n'était pas ce que j'attendais du mariage, je croyais justement qu'un couple, c'était prendre sa liberté avec son mari'.[29] Her naivety did not last long and very soon she felt the need to change things: 'J'avais envie de me révolter, j'avais envie de tout flanquer par terre, j'avais envie de divorcer.'[30] She eventually remained unhappily married for twenty years until her husband died only two weeks before the interview. From that point, she realised that not only was she able to take care of herself and of her life alone, but also that she was getting her confidence back after decades of low self-esteem. According to Serreau's comment about the mourning period of the widow: 'elle était resplendissante, enfin elle pouvait sortir, aller voir des "opérettes"'[31] (Serreau 1978b).

She is very frank about her sexuality and confesses that fear of unwanted pregnancies made her frigid, a state reinforced by her complete ignorance of sexual matters before her wedding night. Her account of several abortions she had to carry out alone (see the last chapter) illustrates what sexuality represented for women of her generation. Far from being a source of fulfilment, it meant nothing but trouble. Unlike the pastor, her main target is her husband whom she sees as the archetype of manhood. After she suggested that he make some efforts to achieve a degree of equality within their relationship, he told her that 'le caractère d'un homme, on ne pouvait pas le changer ... et que des changements, il n'y en aurait pas'.[32]

29 'Marriage wasn't at all what I was expecting. I thought that becoming a couple meant to be free with one's husband.'
30 'I wanted to rebel, I wanted to drop everything, I wanted to divorce.'
31 'she was glowing with happiness. At last she would be able to go out and listen to operettas.'
32 'men's character cannot be changed ... and there won't be any change whatsoever'.

Sexual and social politics

Serreau's initial project was to make a film called *Utopie* in which
women would describe the society they wanted. Despite the
absence of direct references to utopia, one can wonder whether
the project in itself did not sound at the time like an absolute
utopia. The initial idea of giving all French women a voice, and the
conditions of production which were far from ideal, could be seen
as totally utopian. More important, she tried to put into practice
her conception of feminism and Marxism by making a political
statement which allowed for both. Giving a voice to several women
with different social, geographical and political backgrounds was a
way for her to reconsider gender from two initially clear and
distinct axes which would ideally and eventually coincide: the
individual and the collective. There is no doubt that Serreau believes
in the idea that the personal is political. She often emphasised in
interviews that the struggle was double and that women themselves were aware that they have to fight on two fronts. On the one
hand there was women's role in society and on the other their
sexuality and the sexual exploitation of their body. For Serreau,
'apparemment ces deux combats s'opposent, mais dans le fond,
ils se rejoignent: c'est toujours la même exploitation, les mêmes
interdits, les mêmes profits pour les mêmes personnes. Contre
cette exploitation, les mêmes formes de bagarre sont nécessaires
... Il y a bien convergence entre ces deux types de lutte'[33] (Serreau
1978c: 27). She also stresses that the construction of the film itself
illustrates the dialectic of both tendencies with the working-class
women speaking mainly of their collective struggle, without really
referring to their personal lives, while most of the others talk
mostly about themselves and in a very individualistic manner.

Although none of her subsequent films expresses the two
double axes (sex and class on the one hand and collective and
individual on the other) in such an obvious way, there are, however, always some reminders of the dual element (see next

33 'these two struggles seem to be in opposition, but they are actually linked: it is
   always the same exploitation, the same prohibitions, the same gains for the
   same people. Against these exploitations, the same forms of struggle are
   required ... There is indeed a similarity between these two types of struggle.'

chapter). All her fictional work integrates what G. Donnet calls the 'dimension onirique de l'utopie' which is for him the 'symptôme d'une résistance générale à l'inadéquation du désir avec le monde extérieur'[34] (1983: 19). Serreau's constant rewriting of society integrates variations of utopia, from *Pourquoi pas!* to *La Belle Verte*. Another form of 'resistance', this time to the external world, is also manifest in Serreau's second fiction film, *Qu'est-ce qu'on attend pour être heureux!*, made in 1982 and referred to in the previous chapter. The film is slightly different from all the others in so far as the 'community' is more obviously an allegory of society and the social organisation within it. Serreau presents a group with a similar interest (acting) but initially made up of individuals (here artists with distinctive skills) who end up united against their oppressors after being repeatedly humiliated. The reasons for their rebellion are presented in a humorous way but they nonetheless epitomise the power struggle between those whose main interest is money and those they can therefore 'buy' (here the artists who can be seen as standing for those who own only their *savoir faire*).

The power relationships between all the characters present on the set are obvious throughout the whole film. Between the almighty managing director of the car company at the top of the social scale and the powerless artists who are at the bottom, all the 'middle' categories are shown as both powerful and powerless according to who they are dealing with. The technicians/cleaners, who are part of the film crew, are just 'above' the artists on the power scale, but they do not use their 'power' against them. On the contrary, they are the only ones who behave humanly towards them. Although they do not belong to the same social category, the cleaners could be seen as the labour forces, being repeatedly exploited by their hierarchical superiors. The interesting aspect, however, is the fact that although they seem to dissociate themselves from the rest of the team and to join the rebels, they eventually remain on the side of those who pay, i.e., their exploiters. This could illustrate the alienation of the working class

34 'the dream-like dimension of utopia, symptom of a general resistance to the mismatch between desire and the external world'.

in this metaphorical representation of capitalism. The artists, who are marginalised and often considered as social outcasts (since they do not 'produce' anything), would then become those whose role is to trigger reactions. It is exactly what Serreau, whose aim is to 'décrire comment naît, grandit et éclate le refus violent d'une organisation du travail et des rapports humains, où le chaos et le gaspillage sont la règle' is doing in her film[35] (1982a).

One could wonder to what extent the rebellion of the artists at the end of the film could not just be seen as a sort of 'happening' or a show. The presence in the background of a huge reproduction of a painting by the French seventeenth-century painter Lorrain reinforces in a way the idea of performance since the rebellious artists appear in some long shots to be part of the painted background. So also do the 'weapons' used by the rebels: custard pies, water and ventilator, or in other words, all the 'torture instruments' previously used on the set by the film crew. Other elements contribute to this blurring between 'reality' and 'representation': the fake decor offered by the painting, as far as can be from the 'real' warehouse where the ad was shot, the exchange of costumes between the artists who previously 'represented' something (opera and ballet) or someone (Fred Astaire, Rudolph Valentino and Jean Harlow). Although one artist declares that 'les saltimbanques sont le sel de la terre' (acrobats are the salt of the earth), they are also entertainers whose role and function are marginalised in capitalist society of which the set is a microcosm. They recover a control over their performance at the end of the film, denied to them at the beginning. Their integrity as artists is constantly threatened by the social organisation which indirectly forces them, if they are to survive, to perform scripts they have not written, and to do things they despise with people who consider their skills as another product or commodity they can buy. The revolutionary power of theatre and art in general is therefore always undermined by the forces of the market. The testimony of one middle-aged actress at the end of the film that: 'c'est pas ça que j'aurais voulu faire de ma vie' (it is not what I wanted to do

35 'describe how can emerge, grow and explode a violent refusal of an organisation of work and human relations where chaos and waste are the rules'.

with my life) echoes some of the account by the interviewees in Serreau's documentary. The whole film also illustrates Serreau's report, published under a pseudonym, on the world of advertising seen by a female actress. Writing about her casting session for a washing powder, she denounced the way actors are treated, the repeated humiliations and the exploitation, both financial and sexual, that she (and the other unemployed actors) have to suffer: 'je commence à en avoir par dessus la tête de leur spot stupide, mais je pense aux 4000F, et je recommence en essayant d'être amoureuse, séduisante, séduite, drôle, naturelle, simple, coquine, et tout, et tout, et plus ça va, plus j'ai envie de vomir, et de quitter cet endroit et ces débiles qui n'ont rien à voir avec mon métier, avec ce métier que j'aime'[36] (Musidora 1976: 113).

On the other hand, as so often in her work, Serreau suggests the possibility of something else and she often chooses open-ended ends where the viewers can imagine whatever pleases them. Serreau wants to trigger reactions, 'donner au public l'envie de risquer ce refus, pour construire autre chose que je ne prétends pas décrire'[37] (*ibid.*). One can wonder what the film actually and eventually calls for since the film ends with the group of artists leaving the 'stage' of their rebellion just before the arrival of the police and running away. The film is therefore typical of her wish to simultaneously entertain and make people think, a way for Serreau to bridge the dichotomy of Art as seen by the Romantic poets, with on the one hand those who were only interested in the aesthetic side of Art (*l'Art pour l'Art*) while others wanted to make it a useful weapon to fight injustice.

36 'I start to be fed up with their stupid ad, but then I think of the 4,000 francs and I do it again, trying to be loving, charming, seduced, funny, natural, simple, pretty, you name it, and the more it goes on, the sicker I feel and the more I want to leave this place and all these idiots who have nothing to do with my real job, with this job I really like.'

37 'to give to the audience the wish to risk this refusal, in order to build something I do not intend to describe'.

Conclusion

Although this chapter has dealt mainly with the most obviously 'political' or committed films Serreau made in the late 1970s and early 1980s, her other cinematographic and theatrical works express a similar rejection and refusal of the unjust organisation of capitalist societies such as France. The other fiction films and plays she made, wrote and/or performed, albeit less openly committed, are, however, deeply rooted in the long tradition of the quest for social justice which characterises French artists from the eighteenth century onwards. Combining different influences and sources, as will be seen in the following chapter, Serreau epitomises a variation of the humanism reminiscent of Voltaire's century. Despite her repeated assertion that she does not want to lecture the audience and that she is not *une donneuse de leçons* (a preacher), she endlessly gives her audience some food for thought, always remembering like many of her famous predecessors two centuries earlier that humour can be both a unique tool and an effective weapon.

References

Bakhtin, M. (1968), *Rabelais and His World*, Cambridge, Mass., MIT Press.

Ballérini, E. (1987), 'L'Expérience du cinéma militant pendant l'entre-deux-mai de 1968 à 1981: une parenthèse historique?', *CinémAction*, no. 41, pp. 88–105.

Bernheim, N. L. (1976), 'Sujet-objet, où suis-je?', in *Paroles … elles tournent*, des femmes de Musidora, Paris, Editions des Femmes, pp. 36–40.

Chevallier, J. (1983), 'En France: révoltes tous azimuths pour vivre autrement', *CinémAction*, no. 25, pp. 31–42.

CinémAction (1983), '1960–1980: vingt ans d'utopie au cinéma', M. Serceau (ed.), no. 25.

CinémAction (1987), 'Le Documentaire français', R. Prédal (ed.), no. 41.

Cinéma d'Aujourd'hui (1976), G. Hennebelle (ed.), vol. 5–6: March–April.

Donnet, G. (1983), 'L'Utopie comme symptôme', *CinémAction*, no. 25, p. 19.

Forbes, J. (1992), *The Cinema in France: After the New Wave*, London, British Film Institute/Macmillan.

Forrester, V. (1976), 'Le Regard des femmes', in *Paroles … elles tournent*, (des femmes de) Musidora, Paris, Editions des Femmes, pp. 12–13.

de Gaspéri, A. (1978), '*Mais qu'est-ce qu'elles veulent?*', *Le Quotidien de Paris*, March.

Gauthier, G. (1987), 'La Malédiction naturaliste', in *CinémAction*, no. 41, pp. 30–5.

Hennebelle, G. (1976), 'Cinéma militant', in *Cinéma d'Aujourd'hui*, G. Hennebelle (ed.), vol. 5–6: March–April, pp. 11, 26–31.

Hennebelle, G. (1983), 'Les Utopies ne sont plus ce qu'elles étaient', *CinémAction*, no. 25, pp. 5–9.

Jeancolas, J.-P. (1979), *Le Cinéma des Français: la Ve République*, Paris, Stock/Cinéma.

Kuhn, A. (1990), *The Women's Companion to International Film*, London, Virago.

Musidora (des femmes de), (1976), *Paroles ... elles tournent*, Paris, Editions des Femmes.

Ory, P. (1983), *L'entre-deux-mai*, Paris, Seuil.

Passek, J.-L. (ed.) (1995), *Dictionnaire du Cinéma*, Paris, Larousse.

Prédal, R. (1987a), 'Défense et illustration du documentaire', *CinémAction*, no. 41, pp. 15–27.

Prédal, R. (1987b), 'Cinéma du réel: vitrine du documentaire', *CinémAction*, no. 41, pp. 46–52.

Prédal, R. (1987c), 'Des origines au grand tournant des années 60', *CinémAction*, no. 41, pp. 70–7.

Serceau, D. (1983), 'Du messianisme prolétarien à la transformation des consciences', *CinémAction*, no. 25, pp. 118–29.

Serceau, D. (1987a), 'L'avènement du cinéma direct et la métamorphose de l'approche documentaire', *CinémAction*, no. 41, pp. 78–87.

Serceau, D. (1987b), 'Les Jeux de la vérité et du mensonge au service du "bien"', *CinémAction*, no. 41, pp. 88–105.

Serreau, C. (1977), interview in *Libération*, 23 July.

Serreau, C. (1978a), 'Coline Serreau: la force des convictions et le plaisir du spectacle', interview in *Jeune Cinéma*, no. 110, April–May, pp. 1–7.

Serreau, C. (1978b), 'Coline Serreau: à propos de son film: *Mais qu'est-ce qu'elles veulent?*', interview in *Des Femmes en Mouvement*, February, pp. 9–10.

Serreau, C. (1978c) 'Coline Serreau: une contestataire tranquille', interview in *La Revue du Cinéma: Image et Son*, no. 325, February, pp. 27–9.

Serreau, C. (1978d), interview in *Paris Hebdo*, 30 April.

Serreau, Coline (1982a), 'Tentative de déclaration d'intentions', press copy of *Qu'est-ce qu'on attend pour être heureux!.*

Serreau, C. (1982b), 'Entretien avec Coline Serreau', interview in *Cinématographe*, July, pp. 21–3.

Serreau, C. (1982c), 'Coline Serreau: propos d'auteur', interview in *Cinéma 82*, no. 286, October, pp. 40–8.

Serreau, C. (1996), interview in *Le Figaro*, 18 September.

VIDEA (1976), 'Filmer les luttes, les vies, les rêves des femmes', in *Cinéma d'Aujourd'hui*, G. Hennebelle (ed.), vol. 5–6: March–April, pp. 147–8.

Zimmer, C. (1974), *Cinéma et Politique*, Paris, Seghers.

1 Reversing gender roles and identities. Sami Frey as Fernand in *Pourquoi pas!*, 1977

2 Staging the Revolution: the exploited comedians facing their exploiters in *Qu'est-ce qu'on attend pour être heureux!*, 1982

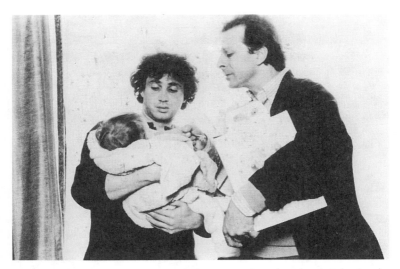

3 'On ne naît pas père, on le devient!' (fathers are made and not born). Roland Giraud as Pierre and Michel Boujenah as Michel holding the baby Marie in *Trois hommes et un couffin*, 1985

4 Rewriting fairy-tales: love beyond class and race. From right to left: Daniel Auteuil (Romuald), Firmine Richard (Juliette), Catherine Salviat (Françoise) and Gilles Privat (Paulin) in *Romuald et Juliette*, 1989

5 Appearances can be deceptive: the 'weak' helping the 'strong'. Patrick Timsit as Michou comforting Vincent Lindon as Victor in *La Crise*, 1992

6 Food for thought: the Rousseauist ecological and utopian Eden revisited in *La Belle Verte*, 1996

3

From the Age of Light to the limelights: Coline Serreau and intertextuality

The use of Art – of whatever form – as a weapon is not new and the film directors who conveyed strong political messages in their films belong to an old and long tradition in French culture. Before the struggle which took place at the beginning of the nineteenth century between what could be called the 'aesthetes' and those more concerned with the social and political power and impact of Art, most eighteenth-century writers were what would now be described as intellectuals. Although the definitions of such a group vary greatly, the term always implies commitment to a cause. Coline Serreau, like some of her contemporaries, can be seen as an indirect heir of those for whom to write and to film is to act, and for whom Sartre would say, 'la parole est action' (to speak is to act). What makes her career both interesting and original is the 'double' inheritance of her work: as well as the wish for social justice (to which she adds sexual justice) and the rewriting of society, both of these central to the work of eighteenth-century philosophers, Serreau also 'borrows' their narrative devices and tone. What also predominates in her work is the recurrent re-creation of micro-societies, in the form of the family and the couple, which recalls the historical, mythical or idealised communities described by eighteenth-century writers.

Starting with the idea of utopia which was the original theme of her first documentary and which is central to her first fiction film, *Pourquoi pas!*, this chapter will therefore examine the ways Serreau endlessly rewrote and re-created her ideal communities from one film and one play to the next. Throughout the last two decades, she has successfully managed to confront accepted ideas and stereotypes about class, gender and ethnicity, and has tried to offer something else. Although there might be a loss of political edge in her last two films – a point she does not necessarily agree with – she seems to remain faithful to her initial beliefs, even if the influences have changed. Without giving up 1970s' utopia altogether, Coline Serreau has now opted for a form of humanism reminiscent of the *Siècle des Lumières* (the Age of Light). A former graduate in French literature, she seems to express the ideas found in many French eighteenth-century texts at a time when literature was used as a social and political weapon and when writers left the royal setting of the Versailles Palace to become 'committed' to the welfare of their fellow citizens throughout France.

Taking intertextuality in its wider sense, this chapter will therefore analyse the direct and indirect influences and quotations from the 'philosophical century' (as the eighteenth century was also dubbed) and to a lesser extent from the seventeenth century. Echoing literary modes of social criticism, from Voltaire's philosophical tales to Diderot's dialogues between Jacques le Fataliste and his master (*Jacques le fataliste et son maître*, 1773), Serreau repeatedly offers new conceptions and visions of 'family', society and communities, which question modern societies as well as the ideological choices they embody. Her rewriting of the fairy-tale to include elements of gender, class and race absent from the originals will also be considered.

Intertextuality

According to Gardies and Bessabel, 'si l'on admet que tout texte est traversé, "habité", de façon ponctuelle, précise ou diffuse, par d'autres textes avec lesquels il "dialogue" par l'entremise de similitudes, d'influences diverses, l'intertextualité vise à étudier ce vaste champ d'interférences'[1] (1995: 125–6). When considering

[1] 'if one admits that any text is crossed, "inhabited" selectively and precisely or not, by other texts with which it "converses" via similarities and various influences,

Serreau's work, different connections can be identified both internally and externally. By the former we mean associations between different texts produced by Serreau herself, while the latter refer to texts other than her own.

Combining genres

Serreau's films can usefully be compared in a number of ways to the *contes philosophiques* of the eighteenth-century philosopher and satirist Voltaire (1694–1778). Voltaire adapted the existing narrative forms of the fairy tale and the picaresque novel to create a new literary form which could express his critique of society in a way which, on the one hand, made it easier for readers to grasp complex ideas and, on the other, allowed the writer to avoid censorship or prosecution. For the *conte philosophique* (philosophical tale) was more often than not an indirect (or even fairly direct) attack on the governing institutions of the day, notably the monarchist State and the Catholic Church.

Firstly, Serreau's films resemble Voltaire's tales in their deployment of a mixture of narrative forms. Just as the tales borrowed from other literary types, so Serreau's comedies adopt elements of various cinematographic types. Beyond the contrasted use of comedy and tragedy which is linked to her desire to entertain and to make people think – although laughter, according to Bergson, cannot co-exist with feelings – another aspect is the multiplication of plots within the same narrative framework, borrowing from different narrative genres ('thrillers', love story, and so on). Thus in *Pourquoi pas!*, there is the false track of the police enquiry, introduced in the early part of the film by the inspector looking for the witness to an accident whose name is the same as Fernand's. Although this does not create real suspense as the policeman seems to behave quite peculiarly, it does temporarily mislead the viewers. The return of the same weird

---

intertextuality then intends to analyse this vast sphere of interconnexions'. We shall employ 'text' in the wider sense of the word and apply it to cinematographic as well as theatrical work.

character a bit later with the same query triggers laughter since repetition is a known ingredient and Serreau's humour – as will be seen in the next chapter – relies a lot on it. The arrival of a police vehicle from which dozens of policemen led by their bizarre boss run to surround the house is a pure parody of *polars* (French thrillers) and is also reminiscent of some of the films of Claude Faraldo – another 'utopian director'. The policeman soon comes back to the house for the sole pleasure of being with the trio. His presence in their community leads to an unexpected twist, since he falls in love and has an affair with Sylvie's (Fernand's lover's) mother. Although the love story between the two middle-aged characters only plays a minor role in the film, it still allows Serreau to show an unconventional couple in an atypical love story. It could also be seen as a parody of 'love at first sight'.

A similar combination is obvious in *Trois hommes et un couffin*. The quid pro quo about the expected parcels (the baby instead of the drug) brings another twist. As well as having to care for the baby, the three men have to get rid of drugs, drug dealers and the police. Unlike the friendly inspector in *Pourquoi pas!*, the police are very hostile to the three men they suspect. In this film, the parody is even more obvious, the three men having to escape the police and the drug dealers while nothing prepares them to play the righters of wrongs.[2] In *Romuald et Juliette* the most obvious influence is the fairy-tale, as will be shown below, with the inevitable love affair between the charming prince and the princess. Yet, the love story is one ingredient among many others and is mixed with elements of social comedy, industrial espionage and white-collar crime. Like the three men in *Trois hommes*, Juliette is unwillingly involved – as an unexpected witness – in a serious affair of food-poisoning and financial malpractice. She has seen and heard enough to lead her own inquiry and, moreover, she has in her hands a crucial document for the case. Although nothing has prepared her for this, she becomes an intrepid detective, spying and using all sorts of tricks to discomfort Romuald's

2 This aspect is much more developed in the American remake which shows a greater respect for 'law and order', since the three American bachelors actually help the police to catch the culprits.

enemies. She sets one off on a false track in order to catch the others, and she disguises herself first as a social security employee, and then as a school mistress, very much at ease in all the different roles she has to perform. Her tiny council flat becomes the 'headquarters' of the fight Romuald and herself are leading against the villains. Similarly, Serreau's theatrical character Maman Lapin in her play *Lapin Lapin* (1986) not only has to care for her big family, but also has to sort out her terrorist son's problem after he is arrested by the police. Pretending to be a crucial witness, she plays a major role in organising his escape from the police station. The sort of mixture described above also carries a trace of the *vaudeville* or farce to be found in films as well as on stage (see next chapter).

La Belle Verte also offers a mixture of science fiction and the fantastic which previously appeared in Serreau's plays *Lapin Lapin* and *Quisaitout et Grobêta*. In the former, the youngest son of the Lapin's family is an alien who at the end of the play transforms soldiers into female dancers. In the latter, the female protagonist is resurrected and is surrounded by a group of angels. Similarly, in *La Belle Verte* Mila (Serreau herself), thanks to her 'magical' powers 'disconnects', among other people, a football team who start an improvised ballet in the middle of the match.

The inheritance of the Enlightenment: rewriting society

Another feature of the 'philosophical tale' was the extensive use of irony and satire, which is obvious in Voltaire's most well-known tales *Candide* (1758–59) and *Zadig* (1747). Although realism was not the author's prime concern, eighteenth-century readers could easily identify those characters who were hidden behind the fictitious ones. They were allegorical figures who represented ideas and notions of the time. The situations they were in were conceived as a means of expressing the writer's views on specific topics. As in traditional novels, descriptions alternated with dialogues reminiscent of the Greek philosophical exchanges where philosophical dilemmas were exposed and discussed. For the *Encyclopédie*, a major eighteenth-century work (1751–72) which was a huge philosophical dictionary in seventeen volumes edited by Diderot, the *conte* (tale) is defined as 'un récit fabuleux ... dont le mérite principal consiste en la variété et la vérité des peintures, la finesse et la plaisanterie, la vivacité et la convenance du style, le contraste piquant des événements ... Son but est moins d'instruire que d'amuser'.[3] This definition might equally aptly be applied to Serreau's work, although the targets for her critique are clearly somewhat different from Voltaire's.

In *Pourquoi pas!* the ideas and concepts dealt with by the main characters are of both a sexual and a social nature. Although none of them are the objects of explicit discussion in the film, these ideas do question the accepted conceptions of the main audience on the subject. Coline Serreau confronts traditional stereotypes about gender roles and class by placing a bisexual working-class man (Fernand/Sami Frey) in the situation of a housewife while a former middle-class housewife (Alex/Christine Murillo) is the breadwinner of the community composed of herself, Fernand and Louis (Mario Gonzalez), lover of the two others and (emotional) son of a wealthy and unstable couple. The director rejected the definition of her film as a *film à thèse*. It is in her view, 'seulement l'affirmation que d'autres rapports peuvent être vécus'[4] (1977). She described her characters' way of life as the result of former traumas: 'Ils se sont réorganisés, non en fonction des normes de la société, mais en fonction de leurs besoins et de leurs désirs'[5] (1977). Her aim is therefore to reverse the classic plot in love stories, that is the triangle of a man and two women. This desire to transgress existing narrative conventions is a key aspect of Serreau's work as will be shown later. Yet it cannot be considered without another even more important aspect, that of social and sexual rules.

Homosexuality was (and in many ways still is) rarely depicted

3 'a fabulous tale ... whose main value lies in the variety and the authenticity of the pictures, the subtlety and wit, the style's vividness and conventions, and the biting contrasts of events ... Its aim is more to entertain than to instruct.'

4 'only the assertion that other forms of relationships are possible'.

5 'They have reorganised their lives by taking into account their own desires and needs and not the norms of society.'

in French cinema where the few films dealing with the subject were often homophobic. A film released the same year as *Pourquoi pas!* is a perfect example of such a tradition. *La Cage aux folles*, directed by Edouard Molinaro, is a film which offers a very conservative view of homosexuality by setting the story in the apparently unconventional household of a drag queen and his/her lover. Conceived as a comedy, the film laughs at and mocks the drag queen whose behaviour is outrageously described. It also keeps the characters in a limited and marginalised world which is never mixed with 'normality'. There is no apparent wish to make the characters and their lives acceptable to the audience, and they are never presented as an alternative to the dominant representation of sexuality.

On the contrary and far from such conventions, Coline Serreau aspires to show that sexuality can be lived differently. Fourier's phalanstery seen in the previous chapter, where society is organised according to its members' needs and desires and where harmony reigns supreme, very much inspires her ideal and yet possible community. Fernand, Alex and Louis have succeeded in creating their own society, a community with its own rules. They live in a semi-utopian community where ownership is absent and where the 'rules' are based on each of the members' skills. Far from the capitalist organisation of society relying on a social, sexual and economic hierarchy and imposing prohibitions, the trio live innocently and ignore taboos, their closeness reinforced by the choice of shots used in the film. The camera always seems to follow the characters closely and most of the shots are medium or close-ups. Although they are still confronted by the rest of the world and have to face rejection from those they have left (Fernand's ex-wife, Alex's ex-husband and Louis's parents), the power and the strength of their happiness are such that they affect all those who enter their Icarian world. The three 'intruders' who, temporary or not, join their circle represent a different side of 'normal' society. First there is the policeman who penetrates their sphere by chance and cannot help coming back; then Fernand's new middle-class lover Sylvie whose initial conceptions of traditional heterosexual couple and gender roles are watered down at the end of the film when she decides to stay despite her discovery of Fernand's sexual life with his house mates; finally, Sylvie's mother, initially presented as a typical *bourgeoise* (reminiscent in many ways of the middle-class woman inter-viewed in *Mais qu'est-ce qu'elles veulent?* as she 'quotes' some of her comments about gender roles) who starts a romantic affair with the policeman when she comes to visit her daughter.[6] Whatever they stand for from a social or a sexual perspective, all the outsiders end up either staying or being influenced by the trio's way of life. Sylvie's choice at the end of the film could easily be read as an indirect invitation to anyone interested to join what is now a foursome. This does not mean, however, that Serreau judges Sylvie's previous life as the film is a direct call for tolerance. This is another key feature of the director's work since all her cinematographic and theatrical texts repeatedly offer alternatives to the dominant models of family and couple (as will be seen in Chapter 5), but also to accepted forms of social categorisation.

Her next film, *Qu'est-ce qu'on attend pour être heureux!* (1982) ends up in a similar fashion, since it is a sort of catalyst for the audience. Indeed, Serreau declared that 'mon histoire s'arrête alors que seul le germe de ce qui pourrait être autrement est planté dans le cœur des personnages'[7] (1982). Again Fourier's phalanstery seems an obvious influence behind the apparent chaos of the film set. What Serreau denounces is the lack of labour organisation which does not take into account the workers' skills. As Nathanaël, one of the pseudo *clown tzigane* (gipsy clowns) performed by Coline's brother Dominique, says: 'On nous demande tout le temps de faire des choses qu'on sait pas faire et ce qu'on sait faire, personne n'en veut'.[8] The last sequences of the film show the artists doing what they are good at and enjoy doing, each performing for his, her and their pleasure only. Although some of

6 This is not the only example of a love affair between middle-aged people. Examples can be found in all her films save *Trois hommes et un couffin* (unless one considers Jacques's mother and her girlfriend as one).

7 'my story stops while only the germ of what could be different is planted deep inside the heart of the characters'.

8 'We are asked all the time to do things we can't do and no one wants what we are actually good at.'

them knew each other before, they had previously arrived separately, often in pairs, and each group was involved in its own problems. They end up leaving the set together in the technicians' van, united in their struggle and in their common interest for their varied arts.

Domestic space as a microcosm

Although *Trois hommes et un couffin* (1985) seems more concerned with the rewriting of masculinity and father/motherhood, it also confronts traditional conceptions of society and roles within it. The 'community' created by the three bachelors could be seen as another alternative to accepted gender roles, and a variation of the ideal society created by the trio of *Pourquoi pas!* The main difference is that, unlike Fernand and his lovers whose relationship is of an emotional nature, the three men initially decided to share the same space for economic reasons and, until the arrival of the baby, they all lead very individualistic lives. The 'intruder' Marie brings initial chaos to the bachelors' household, but her presence also generates new bonds between the men who eventually learn to care for someone other than themselves. They also learn to live with each other in a much more constructive way since they have to organise a rota system to foster the baby, and to use each other's skills to give it the best possible environment.

Far from remaining the clearly divided space between the men that their flat initially was, their home becomes a common space in some ways reminiscent of the sunny suburban villa of *Pourquoi pas!* After presenting each man doing his own business in his own 'domain', the film then shows them interacting in a less and less identified space. More emphasis is given to the common rooms such as the lounge, the bathroom and the kitchen where the three men meet the baby's needs. After the series of long tracking shots showing the men moving from one room to the next and along what appear as endless corridors, the camera gets closer and offers medium shots and close-ups of the male protagonists and of the baby. The 'magical spell' of the phalansterians' house in *Pourquoi pas!* is, however, absent from the three men's house, since all the 'intruders' are rejected. From the policemen to the nurse or the caretaker, they are all kept at bay from the main stage. The space is restricted in such a way that the film could easily be a play. Slamming doors and hectic behaviour from the protagonists also remind the audience of farce or *vaudeville*. More than in *Pourquoi pas!* where the main characters were seen outside their sphere, the three men live and act within the confined space of their flat.

Although a lot could be said – and has been said by American feminists such as Tania Modleski – on both the original film and its American remake, about women's absence within the narrative and their presence only through a miniature female replica or as infantilised adults (1988), the film appears to end up with a new community whose centre is the baby. It offers the 'selfish' men a focal point from which they all reconsider their lives and their sexual and gender identity. The departure of the baby earlier in the narrative had brought another form of chaos into their lives. They then found themselves in the position they were in at the beginning of the film, as free and footloose bachelors, but far from bringing them the pleasures they were used to, the situation makes them realise how empty and unfulfilled their previous life was. Initially unable to share their inner thoughts with each other, they gradually manage to express their feeling of loss and eventually to behave with the baby in front of each other in a way which was until then very secretive. Serreau still considers that this film is her most feminist one.

Beyond class and race

With *Romuald et Juliette*, Coline Serreau includes another element, until then absent from her films and plays (except the documentary *Grand-mères de l'Islam* made in 1978), which is the 'ethnic Other'. In her first films she had shown mainly an ethnically uniform French society, before starting at the end of the 1980s to introduce in a more direct way other social and ethnic groups. Thus, she reflects social changes and its consequences (white- and blue-collar delinquency and drugs in *Romuald et Juliette*, unemployment and social exclusion in *La Crise*), with the arrival of a pluri-ethnic French society. At a time when racism was becoming a wider problem fuelled among other things by the rise of the far-right political party Front National (National Front) who had won a local election in Dreux in 1983 and whose electoral support was rising fast, she rewrote the almost universal myth of Romeo and Juliette, giving Juliette a different age, class and ethnic identity from the original.

Like Voltaire who 'adapted' some aspects of the fairy-tale to express his philosophical ideas, from the beginning of *Candide* reminiscent of the 'il était une fois' (once upon a time) to his Proppian characters (see below), Serreau transforms the myth into a comedy while using some ingredients typical of the fairy-tale. Indeed, in this comedy, one can identify some elements of the fairy-tale as described by Wladimir Propp in his study of the folk-tale: the male hero follows the same situation, and is surrounded by the same *actants* (acting agents) as the ones described by the Russian formalist. Propp analysed Russian folk-tales and found many similarities between them. This allowed him to classify characters according to their function within the narrative. He identified eight recurring roles: the hero or victim, the false hero, the princess and her father, the villain, the donor, the helper and the dispatcher. He then analysed the situations offered to the characters and found that they were limited (he suggested 31) and could be classified under wider headings: the preparation followed by the complication, the transference, the struggle, the return, and eventually the recognition. One interesting aspect of the film is that while the managing director of the firm Blanlait Romuald Blindet can easily take the part of the handsome prince, Juliette (Madame Bonaventure, the cleaning woman of the firm) could be seen as both the good fairy and the princess. For she is not only the one Romuald ends up loving but she is also at the beginning the helper and the donor. Even if they are sometimes combined in a single character, Propp's character functions apply to the film and reveal the senses in which Serreau – like Voltaire – draws on traditional narrative structures. In the phase described by Propp as the 'preparation', 'the villain' (Blache and Cloquet in the film) tries to deceive the victim to get possession of him or his belongings. Then, according to Propp, follows the departure of the hero from home after he is attacked and unjustly accused by the villain. The hero later receives a 'magical agent' or a helper. In the film, Juliette's surname – Bonaventure – suggests her 'magical' power as she can *see* while Romuald's – Blindet = blind? – implies the opposite.[9] After using the magical agent, the hero can then defeat the villain, return home, expose the villain and punish him before marrying the princess (Juliette).

However, despite being far from realistic in the way she depicts her characters and constructs her narrative, Coline Serreau still manages to say a lot about contemporary French society, in a way which is strongly reminiscent of the philosophical tale as described above. For *Romuald et Juliette* is deeply rooted in a specific and recognisable French social context. Her characters could easily be seen as allegories of the 'oppressor' (with social, cultural and economical power) and the 'oppressed' (who lack it), or in more Marxist terms, the *patronat* and the working class, with all the distinctive features of wealth for one and poverty for the other. In a decade (the golden 1980s) when the gap between rich and poor was becoming visible again, and when the euphemistic *nouveaux pauvres* (new poor) was widely used to describe those who were not entitled to social benefits, she shows up social and economic inequalities, albeit in a humorous way. Her choice of jazz music throughout the film, which she described to me as 'la musique des esclaves' (slave music), reinforces what the images show. Despite this statement, the music also has in my view the power to 'de-dramatise' the image, a point which will be developed in the last chapter.

Although she softens racial and social issues (only one secondary character, who is evidently one of the 'villains', speaks in a racist way), Serreau directly denounces the world of business and the pitiless conduct of managers, Romuald included. While he

9 Although this reading of Romuald's name might not be immediately obvious for a French audience, Romuald's explanation to his solicitor that he has just recovered from an 'eye sight' problem reinforces this interpretation.

epitomises the restless and reckless behaviour of the powerful who reject human qualities and whose main concern is profit, Juliette at the other end of the social spectrum represents all the humanity he initially lacks. Despite her poverty, her difficult familial and social situation (she is a black single mother, with five children by five different fathers, who works at night as a cleaning woman and lives in a remote and poor area), she illustrates the merit and values of the 'deserving poor'. Far from the model of the superwoman which was still flourishing in woman's magazines at the time, she shows great strength and courage by not only raising her children while working, but also by sorting out her boss's problems. Like Maman Lapin, the mother Coline Serreau performed in her play *Lapin Lapin* a couple of years before (1986), Juliette cares for her family in a deprived urban setting, very like the council estate where the Lapin family lives. The warmth and conviviality of Juliette's crowded and underequipped household contrast with Romuald's luxurious apartment where no one really communicates, an aspect reinforced by the choice of shots from one house to the next (see next chapter). From the parents who are both having extra-marital affairs, to the children whose relationship with their progenitors seems limited to money, the Blindets' house is a space where its inhabitants never really meet. Juliette's place becomes a refuge for Romuald once he is forced to hide.

Using the well-known scheme of the 'weak' helping the 'strong' in a way reminiscent of La Fontaine's *Le Lion et la Souris* (*The Lion and the Rat*, an earlier 'moral tale' from the seventeenth century), Serreau shows the irony of the situation since it is only thanks to Juliette that Romuald gets his job and his reputation back. Via the character of Juliette, Serreau reinforces one of the film's messages related to women's role and power (or lack of) within society. When Romuald asks Juliette why she has not remarried (after her five previous failed marriages), adding that she needs a man, Juliette calmly replies that it is the other way round. Although Juliette could be seen as having only the domestic power inside the house and over the family members typical of patriarchal societies, she is also the only strong – and sympathetic – female character in the film. All the other women rely on men either financially or emotionally. Thus Romuald's unhappy – and adulterous – wife, who seems to stay with him for economic reasons, or even his secretary who while being his mistress mainly for pecuniary interests becomes a double agent when she is offered some extra cash. Juliette, on the contrary, is far from the social and sexual game. Like Maman Lapin, she has already enough to deal with, from her financial worries to her oldest son's drug problems. In both the play and the film, the harsh lives of the two 'super mothers' still leave space for humour, and their households seem more joyful than the Blindets'. In her 'social comedy', Serreau also manages to introduce 'social-fiction': the insider dealing in *Romuald et Juliette* preceded a major financial scandal at the stock exchange which involved close friends of the then President of the Republic François Mitterrand, and was soon to be called the 'Péchiney affair'.

The last sequences of the film offer – as in *Qu'est-ce qu'on attend pour être heureux!* – a happy gathering of most of the – 'good' – characters. Once the villains are locked away, literally and/or symbolically, the party can start and all the kind and honest characters of different social class, ethnic identity and gender can meet. Romuald and Juliette's wedding epitomises this wish to transcend all boundaries, which is pushed even further when Juliette's pregnancy is revealed in some of the last shots. The final images of a garden party symbolise the ideal community to come, expressed through the solidarity between Romuald's wives (ex and present) and Juliette's husbands, and between generations (Romuald's children playing with Juliette's), not forgetting the presence of Romuald's driver and the housing department deputy played – incidentally – by Coline's second brother Nicolas.

Society and individual in crisis

The main character of *La Crise* (1992) is quite similar to Romuald. Victor, successful lawyer in a big firm, seems to have a lot in common with the managing director of Blanlait. From his social status to his physical features, Victor (Vincent Lindon) recalls

Romuald (Daniel Auteuil). In Ginette Vincendeau's view, 'Serreau's men are "ordinary" bourgeois Parisians ... dark haired, of average height, handsome in a non-threatening way, they are perfect specimens of the average (bourgeois) Frenchman' (1994: 26–8). Like Romuald, Victor is married with two children, a boy and a girl, and the family lives in a big sunny flat in Paris. Yet, the golden 1980s are over, and Victor (whose first name, etymologically, ironically means vanquisher) is made redundant for the main reason that he is too good at his job, and therefore too expensive for the firm. The irrationality of the equation is not the only illogical problem Victor has to face. Everything around him seems to be collapsing. Before learning about his redundancy, Victor discovers the departure of his wife. Then, a bit later, he finds out that the older generation is also affected by the general crisis since his mother has decided to run away with her lover. In the first ten minutes of the film, Victor loses most of what he previously had, and starts a symbolical long journey of discovery during which he learns about life. The rapidity of the crisis matches in a sense the fast rhythm of his previous life. After the storm, Serreau seems to suggest, one has to stop, think and reconsider what is left and what to do next.

While trying to forget his sorrow in a café, Victor meets Michou, a poor and overweight working-class man he buys a drink for in order to have company. Michou is as different from Victor as Juliette was from Romuald. Living on a council estate, on state benefit, he is an unemployed orphan who was brought up by his brother and his Algerian sister-in-law who is dying of cancer. The contrast between Victor's and Michou's daily lives and ordeals is striking, although it takes a little while before we find out about his miserable life. For Victor is so obsessed by his own problems that he is completely unable to listen to others. From the moment they meet, Michou follows Victor who is so desperate that, despite his growing irritation with Michou's presence, he cannot get rid of him. The duo recall Voltaire's Candide and Pangloss (the 'ignorant' and the 'wise') and the social distance between them also recalls Diderot's servant-and-master duo in *Jacques le fataliste et son maître*. It is also strongly reminiscent of the theatrical characters Serreau created in the eponymous play she wrote and staged in 1993, *Quisaitout et Grobêta* (two made-up names which could be translated as Knowall and Silly Billy). In all the work cited above, there is a similar duo with similar social differences. There is also the recurrent contrast between the man who knows (or more precisely who thinks he knows) and the stupid or ignorant (or the one presented as such) – though things are not exactly as they look and the 'ignorant' has often a lot to teach the 'wise'. From one text to the next, the same lesson seems to emerge: knowledge is not necessarily the unique possession of those who are on top of the social scale, and the dispossessed have a lot more to teach and to give them. Since the element of tale is very strong in both films, the 'moral' recalls La Fontaine's lesson at the end of *Le Lion et la Souris* that 'on a toujours besoin d'un plus petit que soi' (one always needs someone smaller than oneself).[10]

It could also suggest what the 'moral' of *Romuald et Juliette* implied, that there are more important things in life than social power and money. Michou's comment to Victor that, despite the fact that he buys him drinks and food, Victor needs him more than the other way round is reminiscent of Juliette's remarks about men. As in her previous film, Serreau shows that happiness is not necessarily linked to money, since Michou's house, despite the scarcity of money and the poverty of the environment, seems more cheerful than all the middle-class homes Michou visits with Victor. In Juliette's and Michou's tiny council flats, the inhabitants communicate and share their joys and sorrows. As in *Romuald et Juliette* where the surnames of the leading characters already suggest the opposition, Michou *sees*, while Victor is blind insofar as he cannot see what is around him, from his wife's depression to other people's ordeals. From the moment Michou tells him that Victor needs him more than the other way round, Victor starts to see. Several shots show him at the station where Michou has left him, wandering around, aware for the first time of the presence of the tramps and homeless people living there. For

10 The translation suggested by E. Wright is as follows: 'there is none so small but you his aid may need' (de La Fontaine 1975: 44).

the first time in the film, the camera shows what Victor sees rather than Victor. From then on, he seems to change, to become more open-minded and tolerant, to accept that he knows nothing. He also stops being the focal point of the shots and is shown in long shots, a tendency indirectly 'announced' by the extreme long shot of the chain of mountains he watches after climbing with Isabelle and Michou. The use of this type of shot is extremely rare in Serreau's fiction films until *La Belle Verte*.

The unbalanced duo of Victor and Michou remains together for most of the film, like Quisaitout and Grobêta in the play. Using the cinematographic and literary classic tradition of the comic situation generated by a pair of contrasted characters, Serreau exploits all the ingredients typical of the genre. She emphasises the oppositions between the two men, from their social status and physical appearance to their class-determined language and behaviour. Their names also connote physical and mental differences, and the nicknames of the play could easily be transposed to the cinematographic protagonists of *La Crise*. As in *Quisaitout et Grobêta*, both men epitomise Bakhtin's (1968) distinction between the 'classical' and the 'grotesque' body, and each is at one extreme of the bodily stratum defined by Bakhtin. He distinguished the 'upper' and the 'lower' stratum which delimit the classical and the grotesque body respectively. The 'upper' refers to the higher part of the body and more especially the brain – in other words, the faculties of reason – while the 'lower' suggests the 'orifices' and 'protuberances'. The emphasis is on Victor's and Quisaitout's knowledge and mastery of unwritten social rules of behaviour and language, while Michou and Grobêta are frequently seen and heard as typical of the carnivalesque body as identified by Bakhtin. The accent is put on their '"market-speech" in language [and on their] rejection of social decorum and politeness' (Stam 1989: 94). There are also constant references to their bodily functions, such as eating, drinking and vomiting, another feature of the Bakhtinian grotesque. Like Grobêta whose character is systematically played down at the beginning of the play by Quisaitout before a more stable 'narrative status' is reached, Michou is initially laughed at and harshly criticised by Victor. His social inadequacies make him an unwilling clown and buffoon early in the film.

However, his sometimes naive and down-to-earth comments actually express many 'truths'. When he enquires about Isabelle's job after she expresses her wish to go to Africa to work with an aid agency (she works as an executive in an advertising company), he ingenuously comments that he did not know advertising was in such demand in Africa. Isabelle's serious reply that she just wants to go there to have a break and a change sounds even more ironical. In a way reminiscent of the old adage *vox populi, vox dei* (the voice of the people is the voice of God), Michou indirectly and unconsciously helps Victor to put things back into perspective. He is not the only one to play this role since most of the other secondary characters directly or indirectly hold a similar function. When Isabelle and Victor complain about their mother's lack of interest and concern for their problems, Michou's comment – 'Ça fait de la peine quand on se fout de vos problèmes' (It is sad when no one gives a damn about your problems, isn't it?) – apparently hits home. Despite appearing early in the film as a racist, he is shown later on in his family environment with his North African friends and his Algerian adoptive mother. Although this could be seen as an ambiguous aspect of the film, as one can wonder what political side Michou stands for, there is a slight reversal of the situation since Victor and his fellow-men are all guilty of another form of exclusion, a social racism directed at Michou. Serreau seems here to mock those whose public stance against racism conceals offensive racial and social stereotypes. The socialist MP is a typical example as will be shown later.

What do they want? Love

In both the film and the play, it is love which allows Michou and Grobêta to reach a superior status. In the two cases, the men fall in love with women from a different – and higher – social background who make the first step. Michou is seduced by a middle-class female friend of Victor's, and similarily, the foreign baroness whom Quisaitout was in love with is eventually attracted by Grobêta. Far from possessing the physical beauty or the assertiveness and confidence inherent in Victor's and Quisaitout's social position, Michou's and Grobêta's main assets are their kindness, their honesty and their generosity. They do not even try to be loved, and they do not even think that they can charm anyone anyway. What fascinates both women seems to be the fact that, unlike Victor and Quisaitout, Michou and Grobêta lack their male companion's arrogance and they do not show off before them. Michou spends the night only talking and listening to Françoise. What is also interesting is the reaction of their male 'friends'. Being loved without 'playing the game' and while being what the others see as a social failure gives the two 'inferior others' a sort of equality until then absent. The focus is then more on the ones who are loved than on those who are not. In *La Crise*, it is from the moment Michou is shown as a stronger character (after his encounter with Françoise) that we learn about his rather sad life. Unlike the direct presentation of his life from beginning to end which Victor unsuccessfully tries to impart to anyone he meets, Michou's life is only revealed bit by bit, and only indirectly. Could this lack of chronological narrative suggest that, unlike Victor, Michou has not planned his life, and takes what he finds when he finds it?

It also triggers doubts about what women actually look for in a man, and what they fall for. Similar questions were raised in Serreau's previous film. Juliette first rejects Romuald because of his lack of understanding and human qualities, and his strong belief in a capitalist society. Despite being a rich and handsome prince, he initially fails to seduce a poor and not so beautiful Cinderella because he seems to forget that his social status and good looks are not enough, and might not be at the top of all women's agenda regarding men. What Serreau's women seem to be telling men is that they do not want to be taken for granted, and that more 'feminine' qualities are an invaluable asset. In *La Crise* in particular, Victor is suddenly surrounded by women who decide that enough is enough: his wife, his mother, his sister and a couple of female friends express in various ways their rejection of their situation and their desire for change.

Discovering the 'Other'

Although the film *Romuald et Juliette* dealt with a mixed relationship (albeit in a minor tone), Coline Serreau also examined 'socially mixed' alliances, a recurrent feature in her career, to be found in *Pourquoi pas!* as well as in *La Crise*. The 'double-act' of Victor and Michou allows Serreau to confront middle-class theoretical ideas with working-class reality. The presence of a 'social intruder' (Michou) within the protected social space of Victor and his like, with all the social quid pro quo it generates, enables her to denounce accepted ideas. This narrative technique is not new and, before Voltaire in *Candide*, another philosopher and novelist of his century exploited it with extreme skill. Montesquieu (1689–1755) used it at great length in his *Lettres persanes* (1721) written at the end of the long political reign of the so-called and self-proclaimed *roi soleil* (Sun King), Louis XIV. Through the naive gaze of Rica, a foreign visitor in Paris who describes his journey and encounters in his letters to his friend Usbek still in Turkey, Montesquieu criticises the French society of the early eighteenth century, and more especially the royal court of Versailles and its courtiers. Rica's comments about his French contemporaries soon go beyond the 'national' to reach a more universal and moral level. The main feature of *Les Lettres persanes* (and of much eighteenth-century literature) is the mixture of comic and moral ingredients, a tendency quite obvious in Serreau's work. The use of an external gaze can also be found in *Lapin Lapin* where the alien son declares that 'je vois tout ce qui se passe avec les yeux d'un étranger' (I see everything with the eyes of a foreigner).

It would be tempting to identify another link between the two texts: Serreau made her film at the end of another political reign which was seen for many as reminiscent of the Sun King's. Similar behaviour by the 'courtiers' and the 'monarch' could be found after a second seven-year period of political power which made François Mitterrand the longest-serving president in the history of the French Republic. What was increasingly criticised in France at the time and from a political point of view, was more *mitterrandisme* than socialism itself. Michou is not Rica, however, and he stands as a 'social other' (as well as a 'sexual other' if we keep in mind his behaviour with women).

On the other hand, Serreau's gaze is quite similar to that of the Turkish traveller. In her film, she offers a sort of panoramic view of France presented through a kaleidoscopic catalogue of characters and situations, in the literary tradition of the satirical description from La Bruyère and his *Caractères* (1688) onward. Victor and Michou witness several individual crises which all reveal more serious problems: the extreme individualism and egocentrism of people who are unable to communicate to others and who are totally absorbed and self-obsessed by their own mini-crisis. From one household to the next, Victor, who is desperately trying to tell his own sad story, is forced to listen to his friends' ordeals, from money to beauty, and from divorce to a broken violin. There is his friend Martine whose obsession with money and material possessions makes her unable to understand her husband's choice to cure his patients with homeopathy instead of allopathy (the latter being more financially profitable than the former). Another of his acquaintances met in a health centre is so obsessed with his physical appearance and his ageing body that his mania leads him to extensive and expensive aesthetic surgery with appalling results (an interesting variation after the anorexic of *Mais qu'est-ce qu'elles veulent?*). It is worth adding here that the theme of *coquetterie* (coquetry), and the attempt to hide the signs of age has conventionally been applied to women rather than men from Molière onwards. As Rica told his friend Usbeck after meeting such *coquettes*, 'les femmes qui se sentent finir d'avance par la perte de leurs agréments voudraient reculer vers la jeunesse. Eh! Comment ne chercheraient-elles pas à tromper les autres? Elles font tous les efforts pour se tromper elles-mêmes et se dérober à la plus affligeante de toutes les idées'.[11]

Whatever the problems Victor's friends have, they see them as

11 'when women feel, as they lose their attractiveness, that their end is coming in advance, they would like to go backwards to youth again. How could they possibly not attempt to deceive other people? They make every effort to deceive themselves and to escape from the most distressing thought we can have' (Montesquieu 1973: 102).

more important than his. The level of self-obsession is widespread
and no communication is possible between individuals. When
there seems to be real discussion, the social game and its rules
which Victor and those like him accept mean that no one actually
speaks the truth. When Victor asks Michou whether he would
follow him if it was not for his money and wants the truth and
nothing but the truth, he is actually unable to handle Michou's
clear answer that money is the sole reason. The only other
characters who are frank with Victor are women: his mother, his
mother-in-law and two female acquaintances. When a political
element is added to the already hypocritical social relationships,
the same 'rule' applies.

The armchair socialist Victor meets conforms to both a social
class and a political party. Still following Victor after his quite
disastrous encounter with his family, Michou is left outside while
Victor and his sister Isabelle visit the well-off socialist member of
parliament and his wife. The politician seems to be completely out
of touch with the daily life of his constituents, and his main
concern is his 'image'. For him, 'un des grands problèmes qui va
se poser en France dans les années à venir est d'améliorer l'image
de la classe politique auprès des Français'.[12] While they are having
a drink, they exchange stereotypical views about French society in
general and the issue of racism in particular. The next sequence
shows the MP's wife and Isabelle in the kitchen discussing and
comparing the merits of domestics according to their nationality.
When the reluctant Michou is brought into the living room by
Victor, the former expresses views which designate him as a
racist, at least until we find out about his friends and family. The
hypocrisy of the socialist couples reinforces what the MP's first
words suggested, that he is an image and nothing else, an empty
representative lacking the concern and care for others usually
associated with left-wing ideas. The 'outsider' Michou unwillingly
reveals the façade and the superficiality of their fake political
beliefs. Like Mila in *La Belle Verte*, Michou triggers and uncovers
the recurrent double standards of the middle classes, whatever

12 'one of the major problems France will have to face in the near future is how to
improve the image of the political classes the French people have'.

they stand for politically. This is not the first time Serreau attacks a politician's discourses. In *Lapin Lapin,* the prime minister shown on television lies to the viewers by pretending that 'tout va bien' (everything is fine), another version of Voltaire's pseudo philosopher Pangloss who endlessly repeats to Candide that 'tout va bien dans le meilleur des mondes'.[13]

'Comment peut-on être terrien?'[14]

The link with Montesquieu's *Lettres persanes* is even more obvious in Serreau's latest film to date, *La Belle Verte* (1996). Mila, the woman from outer space (also half earthwoman since her mother was) who is sent to Earth, is a perfect female replica of Rica. After being wrongly advised about the outfits to wear on our planet (she is obviously one century late), she is stared at by the Parisian population she meets after landing in a public park. Mila could be the author of Rica's letter in which he describes the reactions his Turkish clothes triggered: 'Les habitants de Paris sont d'une curiosité qui va jusqu'à l'extravagance. Lorsque j'arrivai, je fus regardé comme si j'avais été envoyé du ciel'.[15] The same 'naivety' which characterises Rica is a recurrent feature of Mila's character. Her surprise and often disgust when confronted with daily tasks on Earth – while being humorous – also questions what the earth-men and women take for granted in their life. By commenting on and comparing the way of life on her planet with that on Earth, she indirectly denounces and criticises the absurdity of it. Mila's 'weapon' is her power to *déconnecter* (disconnect) people. The effect is such that, once she does it, her 'victims' start to speak the truth. Needless to say, the consequences of her 'disconnecting' politicians and pseudo philanthropists bring complete chaos on a television

13 'everything is for the best in the best possible world'.
14 'How can one be Earth man?' This question refers to Montesquieu's *Les Lettres persanes* where Rica is asked, 'Comment peut-on être persan?', by the Parisian people he meets.
15 'The inhabitants of Paris carry their curiosity almost to excess. When I arrived, they looked at me as though I had been sent from heaven'. (Montesquieu 1973: 83).

set. This is reminiscent of the son Lapin who also has the power to change things since he can see what other people cannot.

The film refers to all sorts of issue, from famines, wars, Aids, and violence against women to social injustices generated at the top of the social scale by the hierarchical and social power based on money and social status, and at every level by the generalised lack of concern and solidarity between people. Unlike the armchair socialist in *La Crise*, the politician shown on television (incidentally performed by the same actor) is not clearly defined politically. Could this suggest the lack of distinction between politicians from opposite ends of the political spectrum? A tempting reading, since the 1995 general elections in France were marked by 'left-wing' ideas being defended by the traditional right-wing party and vice versa. His political cant about his 'concern' for the unemployed changes radically once he is 'disconnected' by Mila. The film also criticises the absence of communication between people, whether they are living under the same roof or not.

Serreau is also very close to Voltaire and indirectly to his character Candide. In a recent interview, Coline Serreau (who played the part of Mila) declared: 'Je suis une conteuse. La parabole, l'allégorie sont des outils extraordinaires pour véhiculer des mythes à la fois éternels et très présents dans l'histoire'[16] (1996). Allegory or 'social fiction' again? The attacks made in the film against a fictitious group TéléArc, which is shown in the film trying to convince viewers to send money to help fight cancer, reminded the audience of a similar financial scandal involving the managing director of the Association pour la Recherche contre le Cancer (ARC) who was accused and found guilty of financial malpractices on a massive scale. The 'disconnection' of the TéléArc leader Monsieur Baratin (Mister Bullshit) causes him to confess his real motives and persona live on television, to the dismay of the producers and executives whom he publicly reminds of their complicity and duplicity.

---

16 'I am a story-teller. Parables and allegories are wonderful tools to convey myths which are both eternal and very present in history.'

'Il faut cultiver notre jardin'

La Belle Verte mixes several eighteenth-century influences. As well as Montesquieu and Voltaire, one can also distinguish some elements of Rousseau's philosophy. Mila's planet, called La Belle Verte, is a sort of Eden and Eldorado whose inhabitants are reminiscent of les bons sauvages (the good natives) or l'homme naturel (the natural man) described by Rousseau (1712–1778). The philosopher shared with other thinkers and writers of his century this conception of humanity based on nature and not nurture. While the philosopher described the bons sauvages and their society before they became civilised, Serreau sets her story after civilisation. Mila's community was a 'developed' country similar to western societies. They had reached a level of technical production which denied human qualities to such an extent that they had decided to give up progress altogether, and to go back to a stage before private ownership was invented. As her sons Mesaul and Mesaje explain, after the industrial era came the big trials and then the boycott. The list of the culprits judged during the trials includes all those who contributed directly or indirectly to the destruction of the planet, such as the food-processing, chemical and pharmaceutical industries, and the arms, tobacco and alcohol manufacturers. Those who allowed them to get richer and who made profits themselves, such as some doctors, architects and politicians, were also convicted. All were declared guilty of 'génocide et crime contre la planète' (genocide and crimes against the planet). The comparison with Rousseau's bons sauvages is reinforced by the encounter between Mila's sons, who land by mistake in the Australian desert, and a group of Aborigines. The same extra-diegetic musical soundtrack which opened the film and introduced the audience to Mila's planet is heard when they discover the Aborigines' group. They soon realise that their communities have a lot in common, from the extensive use of primary materials to their level of civilisation and their 'alternative' medicines. Both also communicate through telepathy.

Like the Eldorado discovered by Voltaire's Candide while he is looking for his beloved Cunégonde, Mila's community lives in total harmony where wars and conflict are unknown. They share their crops, take decisions together and give back to the word democracy its etymological meaning recalling the ideal society imagined by eighteenth-century writers. They have no identified leaders ('c'est personne et c'est tout le monde' (It is nobody and anybody) says one of Mila's sons) and take care of each other. Achieving the wisdom of the Enlightenment philosophers' *homme social* (social man), they came back to Mother Nature and to a natural way of life. Giving up the bad aspects of progress and technology, they have also abandoned ownership, which Rousseau considered as the first phase of injustice in his *Discours sur l'origine de l'inégalité* (1755), and rediscovered human qualities and equity. It could be seen as a twentieth-century illustration of Rousseau's and his fellow philosophers' ideas, another version of his philosophical novel *La Nouvelle Héloïse* (1761) combined with elements of his treaty on education, *Emile* (1762). On *La Belle Verte*, children are not taught conventional subjects like their counterparts on Earth, nor do they attend school. They develop skills either taught by the elders, who teach telepathy and *écoute*, or learnt by themselves. They practise physical and mental games to strengthen both their body and their mind. The *retour à la nature* (return to nature) is also reminiscent of the ecological concerns found in France in the 1970s. Many hippies did leave their urban life to live in the countryside in micro-communities, rejecting towns and progress and subsisting on the fruit of their rural work and often raising goats. They criticised urban pollution and proposed another way of life which rejected the use of chemical energy and encouraged vegetarianism. The opening sequence of *La Belle Verte* combines elements of religious iconography of the early Christians – reinforced by Bach's chorus music – with a slightly idealised version of more recent images of the hippies' communities. The extensive use of extreme long shots showing both Mila's green and ecological planet and the Australian desert is contrasted with the types of shots depicting her landing in Paris. The closer shots reinforce her feeling of claustrophobia and imprisonment on Earth.

This ecological aspect was briefly developed in *La Crise* where the children of the socialist member of parliament from a rural area had declared a mini-war against their parents' unhealthy diet. What they then said about meat and the use of chemicals echoes – or precedes? – what followed the discovery of 'mad cow disease' in the early 1990s. Could it be another case of 'social fiction' if one considers the recent finding about genetically grown cereals? Mila's amazement and horror, once she lands on Earth and discovers what earthpeople eat, echo the appeal of the children in *La Crise*. She is a vegetarian and becomes ill after eating food on Earth. The teenagers' manifesto against chemical-ridden food and their plea in favour of organic food in *La Crise* would probably find many more supporters today. Coline Serreau thinks that the lack of success of *La Belle Verte* is due to its timing. In her view, the film was made too early for the audience to enjoy it, its effectiveness as a 'social fiction' being weakened by its anticipation of recent scandals around the food industry.

Conclusion

Although the French literature of the seventeenth and eighteenth centuries seems to be the most obvious influence, this chapter has demonstrated Serreau's originality and skilful synthesising of a number of inherited genres, from the *conte philosophique* to the fairy-tale. There is little doubt that she conveys the inheritance of the Enlightenment from one work to the next, but from the perspective both of her sex and of her generation, she also offers her audience her own views about society. The subtle mixture of tradition and novelty which is apparent in her work is also manifest in her use of humour.

References

Bakhtin, M. (1968), *Rabelais and His World*, Cambridge, Mass., MIT Press.
CinémAction (1983), '1960–1980: vingt ans d'utopie au cinéma', M. Serceau (ed.), no. 25.
Gardies, A. and J. Bessabel (1995), *200 mots-clés de la théorie du cinéma*, Paris, 7ème

Art-Cerf.

de La Fontaine, J. (1975), *The Fables*, translated by E. Wright, London, Jupiter Books.

Modleski, T. (1988), 'Three men and baby M', *Camera Obscura*, May, pp. 69–81.

Montesquieu (1973), *Persian Letters*, translated by C. J. Betts, London, Penguin Classics (see especially Letters XXX and LII).

Propp, W. (1975), *The Morphology of the Folk Tale*, Austin, University of Texas Press.

Serreau, C. (1977), interview in *Le Matin*, 25 July.

Serreau, C. (1982), 'Tentative de déclaration d'intentions', press copy of *Qu'est-ce qu'on attend pour être heureux!*.

Serreau, C. (1993), *Quisaitout et Grobêta*, Paris, Actes Sud-Papiers.

Serreau, C. (1996), interview in *Le Figaro*, 18 September.

Stam, R. (1989), *Subversive Pleasure: Bakhtin, Cultural Criticism and Film*, Baltimore and London, Johns Hopkins University Press.

Vincendeau, G. (1994), 'Coline Serreau: a high wire act', *Sight and Sound*, 4: 3, pp. 26–8.

4

Women's laughter from utopia to science fiction: comedy and humour

Coline Serreau objected to my categorising her films as comedies since it was in her view a reductive label. It is true that her films do not always observe the conventions of comedy and embrace elements not usually associated with it. However, this illustrates in my view the wider issue of definition of the genre. Although comedy has always been an important feature of early European cinemas, attempts to define this hybrid genre have often failed. 'There is no formal body of theoretical works or poetics explaining the nature of comedy' (Lopez 1993: 55). What is widely accepted though is that 'the pleasure of comedy has been seen as its disruption of convention, overturning commonsense categories of behaviour and reversing expectations. Comedy film therefore represents a genre which refuses to be contained by the demands of realism' (Kuhn 1990: 93–4). The difficulties often encountered by European directors in exporting their comedies abroad illustrate another trait of the genre. Humour does not necessarily travel well, although the visual humour of the silent years of the European cinema overcame what would become a major problem for most contemporary national cinemas apart from that of the United States. The proliferation of American remakes of European films (including Serreau's *Trois hommes et un couffin*) could also be considered in this light, although this is obviously not the only reason.

In France, comedy is probably the oldest and the most popular cinematographic genre. For a very long period it has also been an almost exclusively male preserve, a feature it shares with thrillers, espionage films and more recently heritage films, the other genres highly favoured by French audiences throughout the last fifty years. More than a century after the birth of the cinema, and at a time when French cinema-goers tend to prefer films from the United States, French comedies (and since the late 1980s–early 1990s the French heritage film) remain one of the rare cinematographic genres which appeals not only to French but also to foreign audiences. One could almost say that it has become a 'weapon' against what is often seen as the invasion of audiovisual products originating from the United States. Before analysing in more detail post-World War II French comedy and Coline Serreau's input to the genre, a survey of the first film comedies will make clear the extent to which comedy has been deeply rooted within French cultural history from the beginning. The focus will be – whenever possible – on the issue of gender, in order to assess the role of women in the history and the evolution of the genre throughout the century. The survey will help to identify those aspects of earlier French comedy which influenced her films. It will also show the extent to which she contributed to the development of the genre. Analysis of the role of women in French cinema, minimal though this might have been, will similarly serve to determine the changes which she has helped to bring about.

Early comedies in France (1895–1913)

Comedy is often considered in France as being as old as cinema itself. Indeed, *Le Jardinier et le petit espiègle*, better known as *L'Arroseur arrosé*, was made more than a century ago by the Lumière brothers. Although it was a very short film, it is widely seen as the first cinematographic joke. The Lumières soon had many followers, as the 1897 catalogue of 97 short comic films demonstrates. The fame of French comedy went beyond France as at the time the country was enjoying a world supremacy over other national cinemas, including the United States: 'this particular specificity of French Cinema was openly admired and readily imitated by [them]' (Hayward 1993: 91). Abel goes as far as suggesting that 'most historians would agree that it was the French who almost singlehandedly created film comedy' (Abel 1984: 220). Both the 'tricks' films, which 'exploited the more specific qualities of the medium' (Robinson 1987: 198), and the 'chase' films were highly popular in France before the First World War. In the early 1900s, the Pathé introduced a comedy series starring well-known comedians. The other film giant, Gaumont, was to follow its rival as 'the star comedy series was now to become a crucial strategy in film industry politics' (Robinson 1987: 200).

What characterises these early comedies is the fact that 'most of the comedians were from the circus, the boulevard theatres or the music-hall and they brought their comedy with them' (*ibid.*: 90). This meant that comedies were in a sense 'built' around a character already known to the popular audiences of the early 1900s, such as André Deed or Onésime. This device can also be found in more recent French comedies which rely heavily on a single male comedian (or a duo of comedians) as will be shown later.

The range of roles open to male actors was wide and diverse. For women, however, the situation was quite different and opportunities were comparatively very limited. Apart from the maid, the nanny and the concierge, women were defined either by their function within the family (the mother-in-law, the bride) or by other features such as their propensity for gossip or their 'social' position (the demi-mondaines or prostitutes). The titles of some films illustrate this: *La Course des belles-mères*, *La Course des nourrices* or *Dix femmes pour un mari*. Women were – even at this early stage – excluded since very few had the opportunity to play leading roles (only one out of ten according to Françoise Puaux 1997: 25). Moreover, their physical appearance was frequently the source of humour since they were more often than not over-weight. Interestingly enough, men usually acted the characters of the 'fat ladies'. It is therefore worth noting that the current trend of women as the butt of the joke, whatever the age of their male partners, started early in French cinema. As will be seen later,

Serreau tries to change the audience's perspective by laughing at men. Robinson shows how the young child star Clément Mary ill-treats his maid in the series *Bébé*, which ran between December 1910 and January 1913 (74 films) (Robinson 1987: 202).

This introduction to early French comedy would not be complete without mention of the pioneer Alice Guy (see Chapter 1) whose *La Fée aux choux* (*The Cabbage Fairy*), made as early as 1896, was the first female comedy. Interestingly enough, it dealt with motherhood and fairy-tales, two features which can be found in Serreau's work as will be shown later. It was not the only comedy directed by the most famous French female filmmaker before her departure to the United States in 1907. During the ten years she made films for Gaumont (1897–1907), she made around three hundred films, mostly comedies. One of the most famous comedians of the time, Roméo Bosetti (who initially trained as a circus and music-hall performer), was to act in many comedies directed by Alice Guy.

French comedy during the inter-war period: the *comique troupier*

The golden age of French comedy was cut short by the First World War. French cinema, which by 1914 had reached a position of dominance which it lost to the United States during and after the Great War. Other genres prevailed in the French cinema throughout the 1920s, and it was not until the end of the decade that French comedy came back to the screen. What predominated, however, was not fundamentally different from the early comedies: similar characters to those in the *troupier*'s film (soldier) whose origin went back to the *comique troupier* which 'has a long tradition in French entertainment going back to the 1880s' (Hayward 1993: 151). In French comedy, this character seemed to eclipse all the others quoted by Sadoul (see above), and it is worth noting here that the *troupiers* from the 1870, 1914 and 1939 wars or the conscripts from any period were the key ingredient in French comedies until the late 1970s. Of course this type of comedy excluded women from the start, the barracks belonging – among other areas – to the 'masculine topography'. Whatever the genre, however, the female characters were usually cast in a secondary role as only 5 per cent of the 1930s' films offered a leading part to women.

The *film zazou* and the *film de boulevard* (farce): French comedy under the German occupation

Although the comedy was by and large a minor genre in the cinema of the Occupation (with around 10 per cent of the overall production), other forms of light film entertainment either remained (the farce) or emerged (the *film zazou*). The '*zazou* film' lasted as long as the *zazou* fashion did. The word '*zazou*' was coined to describe 'eccentric young jazz lovers during World War II' (Oxford/Hachette dictionary). For the pro-Vichysts and collaborators of all kinds, however, it meant lack of respect for the values epitomised by Marshall Pétain: *Travail, Famille, Patrie* (Work, Family and Motherland) which replaced in the early 1940s the more 'republican' *Liberté, Egalité, Fraternité*. An interesting aspect of the '*zazou* fashion' was the slight blurring of genders shown through a 'feminisation' of men through their clothing and behaviour. The *zazou* film is recognisable by 'sa désinvolture à l'égard des conventions réalistes ... . Volontairement hétéroclite, il mélange allègrement la comédie musicale, la poursuite, le numéro d'acteur et toutes les formes de satire, de parodie et de pastiche'[1] (Burch and Sellier 1996: 136). An indirect heir of the silent film, the *zazou* film also borrows from the Surrealists either through the musical adaptations of some of their texts (sung by Charles Trenet), or through their refusal of traditional narratives and their preference for the *cadavre exquis* (game of consequences) and the *coq-à-l'âne* (abrupt change of subject). Burch and Sellier see its way of greeting patriarchy with derision as an indirect form of resistance. By denying accepted codes of behaviour, and by

---

1 'Its offhand manner towards the realist conventions ... . Deliberately eclectic, it cheerfully mixes musical and chase film, one-man show and all forms of satire, parody and pastiche.'

glorifying and valuing what was seen at the time as decadent (American music and dance, eccentric and sexually ambiguous clothing, far removed from the virile and 'virilising' army uniform), the *zazous* also stood in opposition to traditional male behaviour and the conventional relationship between men and women. Although it is now recognised that the *zazou* mood influenced more old-fashioned genres such as the vaudeville (Burch and Sellier 1996: 139–41), it did not modify the very conservative view of women inherent to the genre. Deriving from the *théâtre de boulevard*, the French vaudeville on the screen remained, like its cousin on stage, a male-only genre. It is true to say that Molière's successors, such as Labiche and Feydeau, whose plays were widely adapted for the screen, specialised in dramatic forms which fostered the accepted misogyny of French society. According to Burch and Sellier, 'la misogynie la plus constante, sinon la plus agressive de l'époque [pendant l'occupation] se rencontre bien parmi les trente-sept films qui dérivent peu ou prou du boulevard'[2] (Burch and Sellier 1996: 110). Sacha Guitry (1885–1957), a writer and director of such vaudevilles, epitomises this penchant. The reference to him here should not come as a surprise. François Truffaut was among the critics who 'rehabilitated' Guitry in the early 1950s (Siclier 1990: 138). He is seen as the embodiment of a certain idea of the Frenchman especially in his relationship with the *sexe faible*. This makes the recent (1997) adaptation of his play *Quadrille* for the screen by the female actress-director Valérie Lemercier even more surprising.

Another version of French comedy during the Occupation was the 'American comedy'. Since American films were banned during the war, French audiences were given a French 'substitute'. One of the most famous of these comedies was *L'Honorable Catherine* by Marcel L'Herbier in 1942. The script was written by Solange Térac/Bussi. Edwige Feuillère, *la femme à abattre* of the 1930s' films (Burch and Sellier 1996: 54) and the actress who during the Occupation embodied the rare roles of 'strong women' who are

---

2 'the most recurrent, if not offensive, misogyny of the time can be found [during the Occupation] in the 37 films originating from the *boulevard*'.

eventually destroyed, played the female leading part. She was then compared to the American actress Katherine Hepburn, and the film's narrative was quite similar to Howard Hawks's *Bringing up Baby* made in 1938, and released in France before the beginning of the conflict. None of the other films, either typical *boulevard* or pseudo-American, was as popular as *L'Honorable Catherine*.

With the significant exception of Jacqueline Audry, who made a short film during the occupation and specialised in costume dramas and literary adaptations after the war, there was no female director in sight at the time.

From the Liberation to May '68: tradition and novelty in the French comedy

Until the beginning of the Fifth Republic (1958), comedy was the most popular genre at the box office. With well-known comedians such as Fernandel, Bourvil and from the mid-1950s Louis de Funès, the French cinema produced more comedies than the literary adaptations discredited by the New Wave and attracted a very significant audience. Let us remember here that 1947 and 1957 brought peaks in attendances – never matched since – with respectively 424 and 412 million viewers. This thirst for comedy does not necessarily imply a renewal of the genre. On the contrary, French film-goers were attached to certain traditions of vaudeville and farce. Even the arrival of new actors coming from cabaret (Jean Richard and Darry Cowl) did not modify the content of the films. It is worth noting, however, the only comedies made by one of the rare woman filmmakers of the time. Andrée Feix (1912–1977), after a beginning in the film industry quite similar to Alice Guy's (that is starting as a secretary before becoming Henri Decoin's assistant and finally a director), made her first feature film in 1946. The script of *Il suffit d'une fois* was written by Solange Térac, herself a filmmaker who had adapted Colette's *La Vagabonde* in 1931. Edwige Feuillère played the leading part of a female sculptor, an unusual role at this time. This film was an attempt to re-create the success of *L'Honorable Catherine* by using similar ingredients. Although the film was praised in the women's press as a 'woman's film', with 'eleven women in the crew doing the most important jobs' (quoted by Tarr 1995: 116), it was not as famous as the original. Felix's second film, *Capitaine Blomet* (1947), was based on the play by the nineteenth-century writer Emile Bergerat and adapted by Henri Decoin. The actress Gaby Sylvia played the female leading part in a male-centred narrative. Despite the success of the film, Andrée Feix stopped directing films and resumed her career as an editor and assistant.

The main innovator of male-oriented comedy is undoubtedly Jacques Tati. Born Jacques Tatischeff in 1907, he made his first film *Jour de fête* in 1949 after acting in a few films after the war. Far from exploiting the old recipes of the vaudeville and farce, Tati, a mime and music-hall actor, directed and played the leading part of the postman in *Jour de fête*. His originality was to remove almost completely the dialogues and the play on words which typified the vaudeville. He did, however, exploit sound techniques by introducing soundtrack often unrelated to the images. An indirect heir to the stars of the silent years such as Charlie Chaplin and Buster Keaton, Tati developed his genius for visual humour in his second and most acclaimed full-length feature film, *Les Vacances de Monsieur Hulot*, released in 1953, followed in 1958 by *Mon oncle*. His burlesque comedies offered a critical view of the society of the time, from the recently introduced paid holidays in *Monsieur Hulot*, to the craving for cars and for technical progress typical of French society in the late 1950s. Coline Serreau often mentions Tati (alongside Charlie Chaplin and Buster Keaton) when referring to her favourite directors and actors. Tati seems an obvious influence on Serreau's *Qu'est-ce qu'on attend pour être heureux!*, from the criticism of the car and indirectly of consumer society, to the acting of the characters (see below). The two scripts she wrote but never found the financial support to shoot were silent films in the tradition of the American *burlesque*.

The beginning of the Fifth Republic did not bring radical changes in comedy despite major modifications in the French film landscape following the intervention of the New Wave directors from 1954 onwards. In 1958 the influence of American cinema over French production was quite strong, especially in a genre soon to become the rival of comedy for popularity. The French *polars* (thrillers) of the 1950s and 1960s 'were often adaptations of American detective stories transposed to the French context' (Forbes 1992: 48).

The comedians of the earlier decades such as Bourvil and de Funès continued to exploit traditional venues of comedy while newcomers from the music hall, including Francis Blanche and Fernand Raynaud, did not inject anything new. Comedy was much in need of new inspiration but still there were no women in sight.

May '68, the *café-théâtre* and the rise of female comedy

As seen in Chapter 1, May '68 had a tremendous impact on all aspects of French society. For French cinema, this meant greater access for women to the other side of the camera. Although one should not forget that this participation of female filmmakers was initially quite limited, the contrast with the previous decade is marked. What changed in and after May '68 was the birth of a new conception of comedy, and the introduction of women (either as comediennes or directors) at the other 'end' of the joke.

One place, among others, where radical protest was to be found was in the *café-théâtres*, (the nearest English equivalent of the *café-théâtre* is the 'theatre workshop') which proliferated before, during and after May '68. Rather than compare the cinema with the *café-théâtres*, the emphasis will be on the close connections between the two means of expression in the French context, and on the way women could voice their demands.

The *café-théâtre* companies, mainly that of the Café de la Gare, and later that of the Splendid, would be characterised by the desire for subversion and transgression by means of caricatures based on all levels of the French bourgeoisie. What is more, the *café-théâtres* would offer comediennes the opportunity to express themselves on taboo subjects. According to Da Costa in his *Histoire du Café-théâtre*, 'la mode, l'actualité, étaient-elles au féminisme? Le Café-théâtre, immédiatement, présenterait des spectacles "féminins". ... Le thème d'alors: la libération des femmes, la dénonciation de leur "aliénation", leurs grossesses, leurs menstruations, leurs orgasmes, l'avortement, le contrôle des naissances'[3] (Da Costa 1978: 199). The influence of satirical publications like *Charlie-Hebdo* or *Hara-Kiri* was strong in both tone and theme. In other words, what was being expressed on the stages of the Café de la Gare and the Splendid is strongly reminiscent of carnival and of carnival laughter as described by Bakhtin, for whom 'carnival laughter ... is, first of all, a festive laughter [and] it is the laughter of all the people' (Bakhtin 1968: 11–12). So, through the presentation of the body and its physiological functions, 'grotesque realism' would be rediscovered by *café-théâtre* actors (both male and female). Other characteristics of carnival seen by Bakhtin are also useful when thinking of this woman's humour. Thus 'the celebration of the grotesque, excessive body, and of the "lower bodily stratum", the valorisation of the obscene and of "market-place" speech in language [and the] rejection of social decorum and politeness' (Stam 1989: 94) are easily identifiable in *café-théâtre* productions. These places offered one of the few opportunities for women not only to mount their one-woman shows based on scripts they mostly wrote themselves, but also to flout the established order. The transgression was both sexual and social.

The birth of more radical women's comedy dates from this time with Sylvie Joly, a former barrister turned comedian, and Zouc, the Swiss comedian, leading the way. Before 1980, however, one of the demands of women after May '68 was to get underneath surface appearances to show the inner side of things, summarised by Audé in these words: 'les comédiennes, des personnages, des femmes intéressantes par leur intervention au plan socio-politique ont remplacé le mythe'[4] (Audé 1981: 219).

---

3 'if the fashion was for feminism, the *café-théâtres* would present "feminine" plays. ... The themes of the moment were women's liberation, denunciation of their "alienation", their pregnancies, their menstruations, their orgasms, abortion, birth control.'

4 'actresses, personalities and women interesting for their contribution on a socio-political level have replaced the myth'.

Women of more ordinary physique were to occupy a new space, first of all on the stage, and sometimes on the big screen, since many plays mounted by the Splendid Company were to become films. Speaking out was to acquire a new meaning here. Female comedians from the *café-théâtre* were using their body and the physiological functions associated with it as the very subject-matter of their plays and films.

Woman and laughter: gendered humour?

A significant change in the last twenty-five years has been women's input to the comedy genre. Although this aspect should not be overrated (comedy is still only favoured by a handful of female directors, see the Filmography at the end of this chapter), it is worth noting that these comedies have often attracted an attention (from audiences and critics) that few 'women's films' had received before. Is this due to their success both in France (Serreau figures in the list of the top-20 comedies since 1958 with *Trois hommes et un couffin* in 1985, and ten years later Balasko follows her closely with *Gazon maudit*) and abroad (remake of *Trois hommes*, possible remake of *Gazon maudit*), to their gender or to a combination of both? It is true to say that women's participation in and contribution to the genre before 1985 (*Trois hommes*) were limited, although there were as many comedies made by women before 1985 as after. Nina Companeez and Dolores Grassian, not to forget Nelly Kaplan, made comedies, and cast some big names of the time: Brigitte Bardot for Companeez in 1973, Annie Girardot with Grassian in 1977. Their chronic absence from film encyclopaedias and dictionaries of film (Larousse does not mention Andrée Feix, Dolores Grassian or Nina Companeez) reinforces the quasi invisibility of women filmmakers in the history of French cinema overall and in the genre in particular. As far as comedy is concerned, the recent special issue published by *CinémAction* devoted to *Le Comique à l'écran* does not refer to women once, except when male actors perform female roles. It is as if the expression 'funny women' was seen as an oxymoron, at least until the explosion of the *comique au féminin* in the *café-théâtres* in the 1970s.

The fact that women could be funny was, however, not a new concept. There is the obvious example of the successful career in the second half of the nineteenth century of female *cafés-concerts* cabaret artists such as Theresa (born Emma Valadon 1837–1913). An indirect mother (or grandmother) of what French magazines nowadays call *les marrantes*, Theresa (and later Yvette Guilbert) was in the 1860s 'la première étoile du café-concert' (Pillet 1995: 29) (the first star of café-concert). Using her body which did not conform with the contemporary criteria regarding beauty and femininity and using it in a 'transgressive' way, Theresa displayed an early staged version of the *carnavalesque* typical of the female comedians of the 1970s. Pillet's comment that 'tout se passe comme si la mise en scène comique, dans le cadre bien circonscrit du café-concert, de femmes se comportant aussi librement que des hommes, avait une fonction de catharsis'[5] seems to reinforce this view. What is interesting, however, is the fact that, unlike their male counterparts who in the early days of the French cinema came from the circus and the music hall, women did not make it on to the screen. With the exception of Alice Guy and Andrée Feix (the latter's name and films have long been forgotten), women filmmakers never really succeeded in making comedies, at least not during the first seventy years of cinema.

Could this be due to the extreme conservatism of French comedy until the early 1970s and therefore to factors which prevented 'unruly' women from succeeding in roles which were seen as sexual and social transgressions? Or could it simply be explained by the mechanics of the joke and of humour generally?

It is accepted that 'comedy helps maintain the subordination of some social [and sexual] groups through ridicule and reductive "typing"' (Kuhn 1990: 94). One could easily apply Freud's account of the joke to the genre which, more than any others, bases its existence on the device of joke-making. This was done by Kathleen

5 'it is as if in the limited space of the *café-concert*, the comic show of women behaving as freely as men functioned as a catharsis'.

Rowe in her brilliant study on genre and gender. According to
Freud, the joke needs three participants in order to work: the joker
(male), his victim (female), and an accomplice (male). For the joke
to attain its aim, it has to be shared by the two men at the expense
of the woman. The creation of male bonding between the joker
and his accomplice happens against the woman. 'The joke does
not exist until the laughter of the second man confirms it' (Rowe
1995: 68). What then are women's possibilities for creating humour
and laughter when most of the traditional jokes are aimed at
them, when they are more often than not the butt of the joke and
thus usually laughed at? In his well-known essay on laughter,
Bergson underlines the fact that the worst enemy of laughter is
feeling and that comedy needs what he calls 'une anesthésie
momentanée du cœur' (1940: 4) (a temporary anaesthesia of
emotion). This refers to the mechanics of the joke. We could say
the same, however, about the reception of the joke as far as female
spectators are concerned. As women in comedies are the objects
and not the subjects of the joke (just as they are frequently the
objects and not the subjects of the gaze), 'women can engage only
through a masochistic identification with the female victim or a
transvestite identification with the male agents' (Rowe 1995: 6).
This point, as shown by feminists from Mulvey onwards, is valid
for all the other film genres. The choice is consequently rather
limited for women directors or comedians willing to make
comedies: they can laugh either at themselves (which is what most
of *café-théâtre* actresses did in the 1970s), or at other women
(which for Rowe means 'to occupy the "male" position' (1995:
69)). One might wonder if women could succeed in reversing the
mechanics of the joke by starting to laugh at men (another
'experiment' tried by many *café-théâtre* female comedians such as
Les trois Jeanne and Marianne Sergent). Female humour and
laughter cannot be considered without another powerful element:
the motivation of often transgressive laughter. For Rowe, the
genres of laughter when reappropriated by women can be used to
express a feeling women have very little opportunity to articulate
as men do: anger. For Ruby Rich in her definition of what she calls
the Medusan film, comedy has 'a revolutionary potential as a

deflator of the patriarchal order and [is] an extraordinary leveller and reinventor of dramatic structure' (1985: 353).

Coline Serreau and comedy

Bearing in mind the more traditional type of French comedy, what is Serreau's alternative (if any) to the dilemma articulated above if one remembers her indirect involvement in the women's movement and her reputation as a feminist filmmaker? Let us examine a few examples of Serreau's humour in her comedies in order to assess whether or not she offers an alternative to the traditional male comedy, before considering in more detail and from a more general perspective the devices she uses to create humour.

In *Trois hommes et un couffin*, the humour is based mostly on the men's initial incapacity to deal with the baby. Laughter in the first sequences following the discovery of the child is conveyed through visual and verbal humour. While Pierre is struggling with the crying Marie, Michel is struggling, although differently, with the chemist. The parallel editing of the two sequences – with the fixed close-up shots of Pierre's face looking more and more desperate as the chemist patiently tries to explain all the factors to consider when buying milk for a baby, and the wider fixed shot of Michel's vain and hectic attempts to calm the child's hunger and anger – reinforces the humour of the scene. The laughter triggered by the extract is worth considering. Be it visual or verbal, it seems to be aimed at men, or in other words, we laugh at them as they appear to be the objects of the joke. This re-establishes a sort of balance after the very first moments of the film when the three men make sexual jokes about women (including the one-night-stand lover expecting one of the men in his bedroom). However, in the scenes following the discovery of the cradle and its unexpected content, the presence of women in both scenes (that is the impassive chemist with Pierre and the hypocoristic concierge with Michel) slightly modifies the situation. Whom are we, as an audience, actually laughing at? The ambiguity of the comic ingredients in the film makes this a difficult question to answer.

Indeed, after the extract mentioned above, things change rapidly and soon the audience is back to the more traditional situation of laughing at women. Thus the arrival of the potential nanny presented as a caricature restores an apparently lost sense of order. The female audience and characters seem to be 'moving targets' of jokes in the sense that they laugh either at men (rarely) or with them at themselves. Serreau, it would appear, is trying not to alienate her male audience. Does this, however, leave any possibility of women expressing their legitimate claims to reappropriation of the joke.

Another example shows the ambiguity when women are the subjects of the joke. Thus, in *La Crise*, the main character Victor, a middle-class professional who has just lost both his wife and his job, visits his family for some comfort. He has previously expressed his regret that modern couples – unlike his parents – seem to divorce as soon as a problem occurs. He arrives at his parents' bourgeois house in the middle of another crisis as his mother has just decided to leave her husband to run away with her younger lover. Far from being the laughable character one might expect (a woman in her fifties with a 40-year-old lover), the mother (played by Maria Pacôme, *la Reine du vaudeville* who co-starred with Annie Girardot in Dolores Grassian's 'feminist' comedy *Le Dernier Baiser* in 1977) is made very sympathetic to the audience when she explains the reasons for her act. Apart from the quid pro quo which adds some funny elements to the scene (such as Victor talking to his family about a neighbour he has just met outside the house without knowing that he is his mother's lover), the humour relies heavily on the mother's speech and more especially on her surprising use of vulgar language. In doing so, she could be seen as a watered-down version of the unruly woman as she transgresses what is defined as socially and sexually acceptable behaviour and language. She also 'crosses the boundaries of a variety of social practices' (Rowe 1995: 19).

The humour is, however, very ambivalent since the excess of her linguistic unruliness (often repeating 'je m'en fous' (I don't give a shit), or referring to her 'cul' (arse)) which creates laughter distracts us from what she is saying: that she is fed up being a housewife and a nurturer and that she is still entitled to have an exciting sexual life. There is a similar scene earlier in the film with a female character played by Michèle Laroque (an actress specialising in comedies in which she often plays the typical *bourgeoise* going wild, such as in *Pédale douce* made in 1996 by Gabriel Aghion) whose similar linguistic excesses when arguing with her husband mask her real claims. Although in this case, after each 'cul' she utters, she always adds: 'je suis vulgaire, tant mieux'. Through her use of humour, as she allows herself to make a few jokes, Victor's mother displaces other feelings since 'humour gives pleasure by substituting itself for more distressing emotions such as anger' (Rowe 1995: 68). Being a woman who makes jokes, she could be seen as reversing the social or sexual hierarchy. Moreover the fact that she is a mother adds to the ambivalence of the humour. According to Lucy Fischer's recent account on 'cinematernity', comedy is a genre where 'the figure of the mother is largely absent, suppressed, violated or replaced' (1996: 115). This is partly explained by the fact that 'it is difficult to distort the relationship to the mother in a way which makes us laugh' (Grotjahn, quoted by Fischer 1996 : 114). This reinforces what was suggested earlier, namely that humour is in this case displaced. Is the laughter not, in the end, directed at the mother and at her 'foolish' claims of having a life of her own.

It is difficult to decide what the intentions of Serreau are in this extract. One could say that as laughter is gendered (as well as class-, age- and race-related), female and male audiences laugh at different things. What is troubling, however, is that at the end of the sequence, the lover's wife arrives at the house with her children and we expect some *coup de théâtre,* typical of both the farce and the vaudeville. In other words, we seem to be back to a more conventional humour, and the sort that a French – male – audience can more easily identify with. As this extract is probably the most 'radical' in the film, as far as women's roles are concerned, the optimistic view could be that Serreau uses the ambiguities of the situation to communicate her own views. Beneath the appearance and the ambiguities of humour, the content of the female characters' discourse suggests the director's

strong feminist agenda. This point of view is supported by another
sequence of the film which closely follows. This one concerns
Victor's sister Isabelle (played by Zabou, a *café-théâtre* actress).
While both of them are staying the night at Isabelle's flat and
sleeping in the same bed, her boyfriend arrives and announces
that he has decided to move in with her. She starts by gently
declining the offer, and as he does not seem to understand her
reticence, she makes the inventory of all the things she does not
want in a relationship, items which are high on the list of women's
claims for autonomy. By letting the boyfriend express the
masculine view on the topic in quite a caricatured and therefore
humorous way, Serreau seems to allow her female audience to
laugh at men. However, the disturbing element in this sequence,
as in the preceding one, is the fact that here again the scene ends
with a twist. As the suspicions of the boyfriend grow, he decides to
check on his girlfriend, convinced that if she refuses to live with
him there must be someone else. The quid pro quo of the brother
half-naked in his sister's bed provides the vehicle for returning to
the safer ground of the vaudeville. It seems therefore that Serreau
tends to favour the 'one step forward, one step backward'
approach i.e. she draws back from making a clear cut feminist
point, perhaps out of fear of alienating males in her audience. It is
worth noting, however, that together with Juliette – who in
Romuald et Juliette (1989) bluntly refuses Romuald's marriage
offer by giving a list (again) of all his inadequacies (starting with
his colour, his social status, before moving on to his gender) – the
mother and daughter in *La Crise* are among the rare female
characters in Serreau's comedies. The absence of leading female
roles in her films (except *La Belle Verte* with Serreau herself as the
outer-space female Mila) undoubtedly constrains the 'radicalism'
of her humour.

National versus universal humour?

The success of Serreau's films outside France, raises the question
of 'national' humour and the way it works with a French or foreign

audience.[6] It is a well-known fact that humour does not necessarily travel well. French comedies in the 1950s were – and still are – seen as 'inexportable' (Jeancolas 1992: 141–8). The different ingredients used by Serreau will be examined in order to demonstrate what is 'universal' and what is 'national' (French). Some elements could be found in both categories, with variations. It is also interesting to consider the American remake of *Trois hommes et un couffin* (*Three Men and a Baby*, directed by L. Nimoy in 1989).

Comedy, as seen earlier, relies heavily on the 'disruption of convention' (Kuhn 1990: 93). In her films and plays, Serreau uses different means to '[overturn] commonsense categories of behaviour and [to] revers[e] expectations'. Some could be described as universal, while others are more specifically French. In the first category (universal), one can identify: contrasts (characters, situations, soundtrack, and so on), repetitions, comic situations, burlesque, quid pro quo, film topics and to a lesser extent stereotypes (with some restrictions as will be shown later since there are as many stereotypes as there are countries). Most of the elements listed above overlap each other. The subject of each film is not necessarily funny in itself, but is so because of the way Serreau handles it. In the other category, humour relies on the verbal (dialogues) and on the choice of actors and actresses. It is entwined as well with the social and political context, in other words, with all the *implicites culturels* (cultural implicits). These can be described as what is culturally obvious for a native, not taught, but part of a national heritage. The difficulty also arises from the way Serreau uses humour as a means of questioning her audience's conceptions of life, love, and so on. The subtle mixture of laughter and more 'serious' feelings makes it difficult to appreciate her humour. Describing *La Crise* as the story of a man whose life collapses after he loses his wife and his job could suggest that the film is a drama ... which it is in many ways. This probably illustrates Serreau's objection mentioned earlier.

6 Especially when transmitted on European televisions where, as seen in Chapter 1, her films have attracted millions of viewers: 6 million for *Romuald et Juliette*, 4 of which in only two months. *La Crise* has been broadcast many times in several countries of Europe, with high ratings.

Indeed, her films fulfil a double function, since they entertain and provoke laughter while questioning accepted norms and behaviours. Like Voltaire and Montesquieu in the hands of whom irony was a powerful weapon, Serreau forces the audience to confront and reflect upon its own prejudices and stereotypes. She also brings into question Bergson's statement about the impossible co-existence of feeling and laughter, since she does make us feel about her characters' life and ordeals.

Combining traditions and comic genres

The use of contrast is often what works best in comedies, and Serreau exploits it a lot. The shift between expected and unexpected situations and behaviours usually triggers laughter. Yet, contrast can take different forms and have varied effects. While using some familiar ingredients, Serreau also sends subliminal messages to the laughing audience. For example, in the credits of *Romuald et Juliette*, she shows a black woman in her forties leaving a building at night, commuting by tube and bus before walking the last part of her journey to a gloomy council estate. Without the soundtrack, the beginning of the film could easily suggest a social drama with underprivileged characters. Indeed, the musical extract changes the mood and the perception of the images since it dedramatises what is shown. The very lively music contradicts what the images suggest. However, the choice of jazzy blues ('We're Gonna Rock' by Gunter Carr) is not unmotivated, since jazz and blues are 'la musique des esclaves' – to quote Serreau – and the mixture of both expresses the 'tragic–comic' mood typical of her films.

Moreover, after the female character – Juliette – enters her flat and takes one child after the other from her bed to theirs, the rhythm of the music fits with the repetitive movements of each body dropping on to the bed. In the same film, the editing and camera movements also reinforce the contrasted situations. The parallel editing of the same activity (the organisation of breakfast and the preparation for the departure to school) from one household to the next (the wealthy Blindet and the poor Bonaventure) allows a humorous description of the protagonists' environment. It also says a lot about the relationship between parents and children. While long tracking shots augment and exaggerate the space – and also the gap between the members of the family – at the Blindets, the close-ups or medium shots in Juliette's flat suggest the lack of space but also the warmth between its inhabitants. It also creates uncertainties about the whole story since the poster of the film shows the lead male character (Romuald) awake in the middle of several black children.

The use of contrasted shots according to the milieu the characters belong to, is similarly very strong at the beginning of *Trois hommes et un couffin* when the three men are not yet close to each other. Again in *La Crise*, the camera follows Victor vainly looking for his wife in their flat. Although in both these films the camera is in movement and duplicates the often hectic behaviour of the characters, another film technique recurrent in Serreau's films – including these two – is the fixed shot of a limited space which frantic characters enter and leave. The arrival in the warehouse of the protagonists of *Qu'est-ce qu'on attend pour être heureux!* is the best example of such a technique. The humour of the sequence is also amplified by the repetition of the same actions by the groups of artists as shown in the first sequences when cars park near the 'studio'. The same long shots show the driver and passenger preparing their bags before walking faster and faster to the studio. As well as the choice of the cars according to the 'rank' of the characters, Serreau adds humorous details such as the car number plate of the two middle-aged actresses (who have no choice but to be extras for television ads in order to survive) which reads 'TV'. While the film crew and the car company executives are presented immobile on the set, the artists are always seen in motion. The analogy with the burlesque of the silent era is augmented by the funny walk of the characters, often walking faster than needed, and by the custard pie which since Charlie Chaplin inevitably connotes burlesque. Meanwhile Serreau, in typical fashion, also reverses expectations. The classic trick in circus of clowns booting a bucket and pretending pain for the delight of the young audience is shown here 'literally' when Nathanaël, one of the pseudo 'gypsy clowns' (performed by Dominique Serreau), in despair kicks a container after being humiliated by the film director and actually hurts himself. The repetition of the same – or similar – actions or situations is another classic of the comedies from the silent era. Nevertheless, as always in Serreau, it invariably goes beyond the sole comic effect of repetition and is consistently meaningful. It would be too long to draw up a list of all the gags reminiscent of burlesque to be found in this film which, as seen earlier, is also deeply political. Importantly this form of humour goes beyond national frontiers since it relies mainly on the visual. The same could also be said of the political content of the film, since the symbolic revolt of the oppressed against the oppressors is universal.

Unlike what precedes, another classic technique in French comedy is verbal humour and the tradition of comic dialogues starting in the 1930s with famous script writers such as Henri Jeanson and Jacques Prévert, and followed in the 1950s onwards by Michel Audiard. Although Serreau does not always rely in her films on their skilful mixture of slang and poetic language, she does play with words. The rewriting of 'Singing in the Rain' improvised by the pseudo Ginger Rogers and Fred Astaire (although as the latter tells the ignorant director, Fred Astaire did not perform in the film), entitled 'I'm Sinking in the Drain' and co-written by the director, is a humorous–tragic variation of the original. The new version perfectly reflects the situation of the tap dancers, soaking wet under the fake rain while singing 'what a wonderful feeling I'm dirty again' and 'I'm stuck in my mud'.

Beyond the content of what is said, the way it is uttered matters a lot. This links the national with the universal. The hypocoristic language of the concierge with the baby in *Trois hommes*, which recalls the make-up artist on the set of *Qu'est-ce qu'on attend!* talking to her dog, illustrates a variation of this trend. The humour is based on the intonations, the extreme variety of sounds as well as on the recurrent use of 'baby talk' and onomatopeias. In *La Crise*, secondary characters 'mimic' sounds orally and physically, either literally or metaphorically: thus the lover of Victor's mother when describing his previous sexual partners and comparing them with his actual partner, or Victor's friend explaining the explosion of her violin with many 'paf's (translated by 'boom' in the English subtitles). The repetition of words or sentences due to the systematic interruption of one character's speech by another is one more comic ingredient, from Michel in *Trois hommes* to Victor in *La Crise*. None of these aspects are kept in Nimoy's film. In the American remake *Three Men and a Baby*, the humour relies heavily on the casting. Tom Selleck/Magnum plays against type and the contrast between his body and the baby's is often emphasised.

Conclusion

Serreau's films often tend to go beyond the recurrent stereotyping (social, sexual and especially national) on which most comedies are based. Traditional stereotypes usually endorse the social, sexual or ethnic prejudices on which they are based. Serreau, like other female directors of comedies such as Josiane Balasko, challenges them in her very personal way. Although it is difficult, if not impossible, to remove or erase all the traces of cultural assumptions which are part of a national culture, there seems to be in some of Serreau's texts an attempt to create characters and situations which are universal. Despite her use of recognisable monuments (such as Notre-Dame in *La Belle Verte*) or places, her narratives sometimes escape geographical identification and are based on social (and sexual) contrasts as seen earlier. It is not a coincidence that Juliette's and Michou's apartments look the same and also recall the Lapins' flat. What seems to matter for Serreau is to show easily recognisable social archetypes, and to underline the contrasts between economic wealth and poverty by exaggerating and underlining the gap between the two ends of the social spectrum. Like her famous predecessors and inspirations Charlie Chaplin, Mack Sennet and Jacques Tati whose humour transcended national and social boundaries, Serreau's humour, maybe more on stage than on the screen, tends to be aimed at a universal audience. There is, however, one area where Serreau's cultural and national inheritance is obvious as we shall demonstrate in the next chapter.

Filmography:

French women directors and comedy (1896–1997)

1896	Alice Guy, *La Fée aux choux*
1907	Alice Guy, *Madame a ses envies*
1946	Andrée Feix, *Il suffit d'une fois*
1947	Andrée Feix, *Capitaine Blomet*
1969	Nelly Kaplan, *La Fiancée du pirate*
1971	Nelly Kaplan, *Papa les petits bateaux*
1973	Nina Companeez, *Colinot trousse-chemise*
1975	Dolores Grassian, *Le Futur aux trousses*
1976	Nina Companeez, *Comme sur des roulettes*
	Nelly Kaplan, *Nea*
1977	Dolores Grassian, *Le Dernier Baiser*
	Coline Serreau, *Pourquoi pas!*
1979	Nelly Kaplan, *Charles et Lucie*
1982	Coline Serreau, *Qu'est-ce qu'on attend pour être heureux!*
1984	Annick Lanoé, *Les Nanas*
1985	Josiane Balasko, *Sac de nœuds*
	Coline Serreau, *Trois hommes et un couffin*
1986	Camille de Casabianca, *Pékin Central*
1987	Josiane Balasco, *Les Keufs*
1989	Tonie Marshall, *Pentimento*
	Coline Serreau, *Romuald et Juliette*
1990	Marie-Claude Treillhou, *Le Jour des rois*
1991	Josiane Balasko, *Ma vie est un enfer*
	Nelly Kaplan, *Plaisir d'amour*
1992	Annick Lanoé, *Les Mamies*
	Coline Serreau, *La Crise*
1994	Charlotte Dubreuil, *Elles ne pensent qu'à ça*
	Laurence Ferreira Barbosa, *Les Gens normaux n'ont rien d'exceptionnel*
	Tonie Marshall, *Pas très catholique*
	Marion Vernoux, *Personne ne m'aime*

1995   Josiane Balasko, *Gazon maudit*
       Camille de Casabianca, *Le Fabuleux Destin de Madame Petlet*
       Anne Fontaine, *Augustin*
       Aline Isserman, *Dieu, l'amant de ma mère et le fils du charcutier*
1996   Tonie Marshall, *Enfants de salaud*
       Coline Serreau, *La Belle Verte*
1997   Laurence Ferreira Barbosa, *J'ai horreur de l'amour*
       Dominique Giaccobi, *Rien à foutre d'aimer*
       Valérie Lemercier, *Quadrille*
       Agnès Obadia, *Romaine*
1998   Josiane Balasko, *Un grand cri d'amour*

References

Abel, R. (1984), *French Cinema: The first wave 1915–1929*, Princeton, Princeton University Press.
Audé, F. (1981), *Ciné-modèle, cinéma d'elles*, Lausanne, L'Age d'Homme.
Bakhtin, M. (1968), *Rabelais and His World*, Cambridge, Mass., MIT Press.
Bergson, H. (1940), *Le Rire*, Paris, Presses Universitaires de France.
Burch, N. and Sellier, G. (1996), *La Drôle de guerre des sexes du cinéma français 1930–1956*, Paris, Nathan Université.
CinémAction (1983), '1960–1980: vingt ans d'utopie au cinéma', M. Serreau (ed.), no. 25.
CinémAction (1997), 'Le Comique à l'écran', no. 82.
Da Costa, B. (1978), *Histoire du café-théâtre*, Paris, Buchet/Castel.
Defays, J.-M. (1996), *Le Comique*, Paris, Seuil.
Fischer, L. (1996), *Cinematernity: Film, Motherhood, Genre*, Princeton, Princeton University Press.
Forbes, J. (1992), *The Cinema in France: After the New Wave*, London, British Film Institute/Macmillan.
Freud, S. (1960), *Jokes and Their Relation to the Unconscious*, London and Boston, Routledge & Kegan Paul.
Hayward, S. (1993), *French National Cinema*, London, Routledge.
Jeancolas, J.-P. (1979), *Le Cinéma des Français: La Ve République*, Paris, Stock/Cinéma.
Jeancolas, J.-P. (1992), 'The inexportable: the case of French cinema and radio in the 1950s', in *Popular European cinema*, R. Dyer and G. Vincendeau (eds), London and New York, Routledge, pp. 141–8.
Kuhn, A. (1990), *The Women's Companion to International Film*, London, Virago.
Lopez, D. (1993), *Films by Genre*, Jefferson, NC, and London, McFraland & Co.
Passek, J.-L. (ed.) (1995), *Dictionnaire du Cinéma*, Paris, Larousse.
Pillet, E. (1995), 'Thérésa et Yvette: à propos du comique féminin au café–concert', in *Féminin/Masculin: humour et différence sexuelle*, G.-V. Martin (ed.), Cahiers de Recherche de CORHUM-CRIH, no. 3, pp. 29–47.

Puaux, F. (1997), 'Le Comique à l'écran', *CinémAction*, no. 82.

Rapp, B. and J.-C. Lamy (eds) (1995), *Dictionnaire des films*, Paris, Larousse.

Rich, R. (1985), 'In the name of feminist film criticism', in *Movies and Methods*, B. Nichols (ed.), Berkeley, University of California Press.

Robinson, D. (1987), 'Rise and fall of the clowns', *Sight and Sound*, 56: 3, pp. 198–203.

Rollet, B. (1997), 'Two women filmmakers speak out: Serreau and Balasko and the inheritance of May '68', in *Voices of France*, S. Perry and M. Cross (eds), London and Washington, Pinter, pp. 100–13.

Rowe, K. (1995), *Unruly Women: Gender and the Genres of Laughter*, Austin, University of Texas Press.

Sadoul, G. (1948), *Histoire du cinéma français*, Paris, Denoël.

Siclier, J. (1990), *Le Cinéma français de La Bataille du rail à La Chinoise: 1945–1968*, Paris, Ramsay Cinéma.

Stam, R. (1989), *Subversive Pleasure: Bakhtin, Cultural Criticism and Film*, Baltimore and London, Johns Hopkins University Press.

Tarr, C. (1995), 'Now you don't: women, cinema and (the) Liberation', in *The Liberation of France: Image and Events*, H. R. Kedward and N. Wood (eds), Oxford, Berg, pp. 103–16.

5

Family matters and *matres*: questioning gender roles

Since the beginning of her success as a filmmaker with *Trois hommes et un couffin*, Coline Serreau has often said in interviews that she considered family and children as a key aspect of society and of life overall. Although she does not specifically refer to women's role, their role and place in the family unit is self-evident. This kind of statement might come as a surprise from someone who in 1978 professed her faith in feminism and the women's movement, and her wish to link feminism with Marxism. It is worth remembering that in the 1970s some feminists developed and defended the idea of abolishing the family, an opinion less fashionable when expressed by de Beauvoir a quarter of a century earlier in *Le Deuxième Sexe* (1949), and even less so during the early days of feminism (despite a few radicals here and there). French feminism, however, contains a diversity of positions on the family as on other issues.

The other surprise with regard to Serreau, came in *La Belle Verte* released in September 1996 in France, which has all the characteristics of a science-fiction film. It could be seen as a piece of pro-life propaganda and a heavy vehicle for family values. However, the ideological reappropriation of family matters by right-wing and far-right political movements does not necessarily imply that family is in itself a 'right-wing' or conservative issue. One way of understanding these apparent contradictions would be to consider the specificity of France and French feminists with regard to motherhood. Indeed, motherhood has always been a tricky issue for feminists from the beginning of the twentieth century onwards and could be summarised by Claire Duchen's question 'Destiny or slavery?' (1986: 49). This can be partly explained by France's long tradition of family policy which has led to a near-national consensus about the whole subject. Going back as far as the seventeenth century, the first ever series of actions in favour of the family were initiated by Colbert (1619–1683). It would be difficult to prove that Colbert's family policies had a direct impact on the telling of fairy-tales, but it is certainly the case that unlike their British counterparts French princes and princesses not only 'live happily ever after', but also 'have many children' (ils vécurent heureux et eurent beaucoup d'enfants). The influence of this powerful ideology of motherhood should not be underestimated. Is there, one can ask, any alternative for French women to the historically accepted and conventional function of women as mothers, considering the importance of the indirect propaganda in this regard (be it political or religious), and the pre-eminence of the iconography (especially religious) reinforcing the idea of motherhood as woman's prime role, function and duty? It is necessary here to consider the social, political and cultural context which surrounded Serreau's formative years, she herself being a baby boomer (she was born in 1947), in order to assess the influence this cultural inheritance might have on her films.

Feminism and motherhood in France

Early feminists who opposed the traditional concept of women as mothers at the beginning of the twentieth century were a marginalised minority. 'Une "avant-garde", radicale, révolutionnaire, très minoritaire, revendique une égalité totale qui implique de profonds bouleversements des rôles sexuels'[1] (Bard 1995: 22). With the increasing fear of the falling birth-rate in the inter-war period, a first law was passed in 1920 which increased the already existing repressive measures against abortion and forbade the

1 'A very small, revolutionary and radical "avant-garde" claims a total equality which involves a significant upheaval of sexual roles.'

circulation of contraceptive material. In 1923, this law was reinforced by a second one which punished abortion more severely
and augmented the repression against the promotion of pro-birth-
control propaganda.

The influence of the Third Republic's family policy over the
decades following its fall were obvious during the Vichy regime
which did nothing to modify the accepted view of womanhood as
by nature maternal. Through a variety of measures such as according to the *fête des mères* (created in 1926) the status of a national
holiday, or the emphasis on the distribution of 'family medals'
(introduced in 1920), the Vichy regime reinforced the importance
of mothers in the construction of French national identity. French
cinema – which had been accused of contributing to the French
débacle of 1940 with films such as *La Règle du jeu* made by Renoir
in 1937 – did introduce indirect pro-family messages, as the
'negative' figure of the single mother and the illegitimate child
was also recurrent in the films made during the Occupation.

During the post-war period and the 1950s, motherhood was
rated highly and 'raising children was considered to be the
summit of a woman's "career"' (Duchen 1994: 102). Although it
had somehow lost the patriotic subtext of the war years, family
policy was as strong as before. Following Pétain, de Gaulle enthus-
iastically encouraged women to have more children. Simone de
Beauvoir's claim in favour of 'birth-control' (in English in the text)
and her rejection of both unwanted pregnancy and motherhood as
a form of patriarchal oppression in *Le Deuxième Sexe* did not
attract many followers. As with the radical feminists of the 1920s
and 1930s, those whose views on motherhood and women's
sexuality were seen as scandalous (to say the least) were isolated.
Choice was therefore limited for women as the valorisation of
domestic and maternal duties over the 'selfish' desire to have a job
was omnipresent. From government initiatives aimed at keeping
women at home, such as the *salaire de la mère au foyer* (housewife's
wages) created in 1938 but still valid in the 1950s, to women's
magazine articles and surveys favouring and celebrating the joys
of motherhood, both direct and indirect propaganda was
abundant and varied.

The French cinema of the 1950s played its part in the debate comparing women's presence at work and at home, as according to Burch and Sellier: 'le cinéma des années cinquante ... est travaillé de façon inédite et quasi obsessionnelle par le thème du travail des femmes ... Le plus souvent le traitement mélodramatique de ce motif a pour enjeu de persuader les femmes qu'elles doivent renoncer à travailler (et à toute autonomie pour trouver le bonheur amoureux et conjugal), ou renoncer à l'amour si elles tiennent à leur travail'[2] (Burch and Sellier 1996: 258).

Off-screen, cinema actresses such as Brigitte Bardot and Grace Kelly displayed images of a fulfilling and happy motherhood, for example on the front cover of the women's magazine *Elle* in January and June 1960. The example of Bardot is, however, quite ambiguous. Three years after Vadim's *Et Dieu créa la femme*, in which she scandalised conservative opinion by displaying female sexuality as actively desiring, one has to ask what sort of 'message' the picture of herself as a mother conveyed to the female readers of *Elle*. Bardot's picture could be seen as announcing the break between the 1950s and the 1960s: on the one hand, she displays the traditional eroticism associated with French women through a long literary and pictorial tradition with an emphasis on the Lolita-like sex-kitten figure, while on the other hand she is portrayed in the almost sexless role of the mother. Another version perhaps of the catholic dichotomy between *La Maman et la putain* (the mother and the whore)?

The emphasis on maternity was such that at the time even the Planning Familial, created in 1956 to inform and help women regarding contraception matters, was initially called Maternité Heureuse (happy motherhood). The name was changed in 1960. According to Claire Duchen, there was a move towards a greater recognition of women's role outside the family in the 1960s, as 'the emphasis in the mother-versus-career debate changed: the

2 '1950s' cinema is racked in a new and obsessive manner with the subject of working women. More often than not, the melodramatic handling of this theme is aimed at persuading women that they must give up working (and all forms of autonomy) in order to find happiness (be it sentimental or conjugal) or renounce love if they want to keep on working.'

double shift was accepted but not celebrated' (1994: 115). The modification of the *Code civil* in 1965, through which women were entitled to work without their husband's consent, might have influenced this trend. More important, however, was the growing interest in contraception. As far as legislation was concerned, the 1920 law was still in force and some attempts were made to overturn it. In 1965 during his election campaign, the socialist candidate François Mitterrand suggested its annulment. The change eventually came from a Gaullist MP, René Neuwirth, who in 1966 wrote and prepared the law (which was to bear his name) decriminalising birth-control. Parliament approved the bill and it was passed in 1967. This was a first step in a long struggle which reached its climax after May '68 and with the various women's movements in the 1970s.

May '68 and the 1970s

As mentioned in the first chapter, May '68 did not have an immediate effect on women's rights regarding their 'procreative function'. Before analysing in more detail the changes in the feminist perception and conception of motherhood throughout the 1970s, it will be useful to review a few key moments in French women's struggle to implement birth-control and abortion. Feminist groups, including the MLF created in 1970, organised several massive demonstrations in favour of abortion before the law decriminalising abortion was passed in 1974. On 5 April 1971, the left-wing weekly *Nouvel Observateur* published the following statement: 'Un million de femmes se font avorter chaque année en France. Elles le font dans des conditions dangereuses en raison de la clandestinité à laquelle elles sont condamnées ... On fait le silence sur ces millions de femmes. Je déclare que je suis l'une d'elles. Je déclare avoir avorté. De même que nous réclamons le libre accès aux moyens anticonceptionnels, nous réclamons l'avortement libre'.[3] It was signed by 343 women, and included

3 'A million women have abortions each year. Because of the illegality of the act, they undergo it in very dangerous conditions ... There is a conspiracy of silence

well-known writers such as Simone de Beauvoir and Marguerite Duras, film director Agnès Varda and actresses such as Catherine Deneuve and Jeanne Moreau. The impact of the publication was tremendous. It was followed by various events organised by associations such as the MLAC created in 1973. In May 1972, an international conference denouncing violence against women took place at the Mutualité and was extremely successful. In November of the same year the Bobigny trial took place. After the abortion, following the rape of a 15-year-old girl, her mother and her 'accomplices' faced charges and their trial illustrated the inadequacies of the law. They were defended by the feminist lawyer Gisèle Halimi who collaborated in the creation of the association Choisir in 1971 which aimed at defending anyone involved in a trial following their participation in an abortion. In 1973, 331 medical practitioners backed the joint actions of several women's groups and declared their support for free abortion. This led to public awareness of a problem until then hidden and invisible. After the Veil law was passed in 1974, feminist groups resumed their actions. In 1975 a group of women published *Maternité esclave* (slave motherhood) which denounced French family policies, conditions of delivery in hospitals and the unequal distribution of domestic duties. Far from glorifying the 'joys of motherhood', the book was highly critical of the harsh reality of maternity. From all the feminist texts published in the first half of the 1970s, the same idea emerges: far from being a source of happiness for women, motherhood induces women's alienation in patriarchal societies. Documentaries such as Belmont and Issartel's *Histoires d'A* which, like the novel which inspired its title, was also banned but achieved viewing figures of two hundred thousand people added a 'visual' dimension to the debate.[4]

---

about these millions of women. I declare that I am one of them. I declare that I have had an abortion. Just as we claim free access to contraceptive materials, so we also claim free abortion.'

4 The title was a pun on the title of a best seller published in 1954 by Pauline Réage (a pseudonym for Emmanuelle Arsan) entitled *Histoire d'O* which is seen as one of the masterpieces of erotic fiction. The book was banned until 1975 but was published illegally by Pauvert. The 'A' of *Histoires d'A* refers to Abortion.

Feminists were not, however, calling for a 'womb strike' as some of their predecessors like Nelly Roussel had in 1919. They were more concerned with finding another way of looking at motherhood and with redefining women's roles within it. When considering the relationship between the women's movements and motherhood in the 1970s, two or three phases can be identified. While Claire Duchen dissociates the first and second half of the decade (1986: 49–66).[5]

The relationship between these phases could be summarised by the evolution from denunciation to praise (Fortino 1997: 221). Feminism was closely linked to Marxism and therefore, 'in 1970, the family was analysed as the cause of women's oppression, and feminists almost universally agreed that motherhood, defining and limiting women, had to be rejected in capitalist societies' (Duchen 1986: 49). For the MLF in particular, 'motherhood would be only acceptable for women after the socialist revolution' (*ibid.*: 52). The period 1970–75 is marked by the link between motherhood and slavery. The second half of the 1970s is what Fortino calls *maternitude*. The word, which is untranslatable, recalls both *féminitude* and *négritude*,[6] and defines 'la valorisation extrême de la maternité que l'on trouve dans les textes du mouvement après 1975' (*ibid.*: 226) (the extreme valorisation of motherhood to be found in MLF's texts after 1975). Interestingly enough, the emphasis in the texts and special issues devoted to the glorification of maternity is on women and not on children. It is their physical experience which is the central point. Later on, feminists expressed the wish to change the relationship between parents (and more especially mothers) and children. The impact of May '68 regarding the idea of authority within the family is

5 Sabine Fortino adds a third phase which she situates at the very beginning of the decade (1997: 217–38). It was in her view characterised by the recurrent use of *maternité volontaire* (voluntary motherhood).

6 The word *négritude* was invented by black writers Aimé Césaire and Léopold Senghor and first appeared in 1948 in France and its African colonies. It aimed at valorising blackness in a way which recalls the civil right movements in the United States. *Féminitude* coined by French feminist writers in the 1970s had a similar goal regarding womanhood.

reflected in texts which offered other possible links between mothers and daughters.

French cinema and family matters

Before embarking on the study of Serreau and her films, it seems useful to take a step back for a quick general consideration of the treatment of the family in French films. May '68 seems in this context (as in many others) to be a key moment. Until the end of the 1960s (or even in the early 1960s) what was dominant was the existence of a traditional family structure, made up of two biological parents and one or more children, not forgetting the lover or the mistress.

These facts would be considerably modified during and after May '68. The modifications would affect the couple above all. I use the word 'couple' keeping in mind Françoise Audé's distinction when she speaks of the 'métamorphoses du couple' (metamorphoses of the couple). She emphasises that 'l'emploi du terme "couple", lorsqu'il se substitue à celui de "mariage" (l'institution) ou de "ménage" (la cellule sociale de base, gestionnaire du foyer où s'épanouit la famille), c'est déjà la modernité par opposition à la tradition'[7] (Audé 1983: 80). What we will find, besides a majority of films continuing to present the classic structure mentioned, is a form of 'redefinition' of the couple, and above all of the roles and expectations of the partners. That this coincided with the arrival of women filmmakers should not be very surprising. Even though women did not tell only 'women's stories', some female directors such as for example Agnès Varda and Chantal Akerman offered female characters in their films. This was evidenced by the choice of different, stronger heroines, as far removed as possible from the 'fickle and seductive little bourgeoises' of the 1950s of whom Audé writes (Audé 1981: 111). The choice of certain themes reveals a desire to say things hitherto kept quiet (the 'speaking-out' of May

---

7 'the use of the term "couple", when it is substituted for that of "marriage" (the institution) or of "household" (basic social unit, management of the home where the family develops), is already part of modernity as opposed to tradition'.

'68), whether about feminine sexuality, contraception, abortion or rape. Though women have not always chosen fiction to express their desires and wishes for change, in the post-1968 period, some women filmmakers were putting 'fiction to the service of the feminist cause', to take up the phrase used of Agnès Varda's film *L'Une chante, l'autre pas* (1976).

Une femme et un bébé: Coline Serreau and motherhood

An interesting aspect of Serreau's work, apart from the strong emphasis on family from her debut onwards, is the fact that after choosing a cinematographic genre such as the documentary – favoured by many of her female contemporaries – she opted for the one whose tradition of excluding women is a defining feature. Indeed, the excision of women and more especially of the mother figure is a recurrent aspect in comedy (despite a few notable exceptions such as Alice Guy's early comedies *La Fée aux choux* made in 1896 and *Madame a ses envies* made in 1907). It is therefore worth considering whether this is another contradiction or whether it could be seen as a way for her to reconsider gender roles and identities within the traditional frame of mainstream comedies while expressing her view on motherhood.

Supporters and critics of Serreau alike have often underlined the fact that her success was mainly due to her capacity to express contemporary concerns in her films. By capturing the mood of the time and by continuously reflecting on society's changes, she has offered the sort of mirror in which the audience was quite willing to see itself. It is true to say that Serreau's films closely followed, and sometimes preceded, major social and sexual changes in France during the 1980s and 1990s. This could also be understood as a tactful way of saying that she has often changed her mind and ideas. The notion of family in the wider sense of the word (that is parenthood, sexual and gender roles, micro-community) is probably where Serreau's variations are the most obvious. In her many portrayals of varied households throughout the 1970s, 1980s and 1990s, she has identified and voiced the moods and desires of women of her generation. Born in 1947 (which, incidentally, is the year in which most feminists of the 1970s were born), Serreau has grown up as a baby boomer in the France of the *trente glorieuses*. As Nadja Ringart noted, 'le Baby Boom fournit donc une part importante de militantes mais loin d'être un mouvement d'adolescentes, le Mouvement de libération des femmes puise sa richesse dans une grande diversité des âges et des expériences'[8] (1991: 160). The influence of women's actions and concerns regarding motherhood and family (among other things) after May '68 are to be found in Serreau's films made in the 1970s.

The 1970s: realism and utopia

In 1972, Serreau wrote her first script and played the leading part in Bertuccelli's film *On s'est trompé d'histoire d'amour*. In the same year as the Bobigny trial and the women's meeting at the Mutualité, a year after the *manifeste des 343*, and shortly before the creation of the MLAC, she voiced and echoed the debate about contraception and birth-control. She told the story of a young woman who becomes pregnant and marries the father of the child because she cannot afford to have an abortion. The film, which was seen as 'peut-être un des meilleurs films français sur les pauvres' (Serreau 1982) (perhaps one of the best French films about poverty), denounced the social and economic inequality of women confronted with unwanted pregnancies. It was also very critical of the way mothers-to-be were treated in hospitals. Monique Rémy commenting on the film wrote that: 'les parturientes y subissent autant de mépris que les avortées' (1990: 60–1) (those giving birth are as badly treated as those who have an abortion). Serreau was not the only one to criticise conditions of delivery which were recurrent in publications of the time. Annie Leclerc in her feminist best seller *Parole de femme* (A woman's word), published

8 'the baby boom supplied the women's movement with a significant number of activists, but far from being a teenagers' group, the richness of the women's lib movement stems from a wide diversity of generations and experience'.

in 1974, wrote that 'le mépris, la déconsidération de cet événe-
ment qui représente pour la femme le moment d'une épreuve
extrême et cruciale de la vie, n'est autre que le mépris de la femme
en général'.[9] Interestingly enough, this script is the only one
Serreau wrote with an unhappy ending.

In her celebrated documentary *Mais qu'est-ce qu'elles veulent?*
(1975–78), which established her as a feminist filmmaker, Serreau
gave a voice to women who denounced unwanted pregnancies
and their economic, social and sexual oppression as women. All
the interviewees talked about alienation, and words such as prison
or hard labour come back regularly when they refer to their
domestic life. The last testimony illustrates what was often the
common lot of women:

> La contraception, j'ai voulu la prendre, mais mon mari était
> absolument contre ... C'est-à-dire que j'ai été enceinte plusieurs
> fois ... et il a fallu que je me débrouille. Il me disait: tu te
> débrouilles, c'est tout ... Et à chaque fois, je me suis retrouvée à
> l'hôpital pour avoir un curetage, et ça, c'est très moche ... Maintenant
> encore, on l'accepte à l'hôpital, mais au début, on vous faisait des
> réflexions ... Parce que ce n'était pas normal de le faire. On
> s'occupait pas de savoir si vous aviez les moyens ou pas d'élever un
> enfant ... On s'occupait pas non plus de savoir qui vous l'avait fait
> et que l'homme était autant coupable que la femme ... C'est la
> femme qui supportait tous les ... tous les ennuis, toutes les
> réflexions.[10]

---

9 'the contempt, the lack of consideration of an event which is for women the
   moment of a harsh and a key ordeal is nothing more than the general contempt
   for women in general'.
10 I would have liked to use contraceptives, but my husband was totally against it ...
   I mean, I was pregnant several times ... and I had to manage by myself. He
   would tell me: 'you'll have to manage on your own', and that was it. And each
   time, I had to go to hospital for an abortion, and that was very hard ... Nowadays,
   hospital staff tend to accept it, but at the time, they were very critical, because it
   wasn't normal to do it. They didn't care whether you could afford or not to raise
   a child. They didn't care who'd got you pregnant. They didn't think about the
   fact that the man was just as guilty. It was the woman who had to put up with all
   the worry and the criticism.

Gender reversal

By the time she directed her first fiction film the mood had
changed and utopia prevailed. In *Pourquoi pas!* (1978), Serreau
reverses the archetype of the couple, first of all through a redis-
tribution of the roles. Thus, the woman (Alex/Christine Murillo)
works outside while one of the men (Fernand/Sami Frey) of the
trio is in charge of domestic duties (and financial matters as well).
Could it be a precursor of the apparently unconventional household of *Trois hommes et un couffin?* Or could it be linked to
Serreau's desire to transcend the boundaries of gender through a
masquerade or what she herself calls 'travestissement'? While
performing the big mama of her play *Lapin Lapin* in 1987, she
declared that she did not play classical texts, because when she
did, she always wanted to play the male parts (rumours suggest
that her wish may come true and that she will be Arnolphe in
L'Ecole des femmes in 1998). She added: 'Une femme peut repré-
senter un homme et un homme une femme sans avoir besoin
d'être homosexuel. Le travesti n'est pas une convention du passé,
c'est une liberté balayée par les conventions imbéciles du
naturalisme, et qu'on devrait être en mesure de retrouver, en ce
moment'[11] (Serreau 1986). One of the sons of the Lapin family, as
seen earlier, does transform male soldiers into female ballet
dancers. Although Serreau played a male valet in her 1993 play
Quisaitout et Grobêta, in which she disguised herself in what looks
like the character of an almost sexless clown (although Grobêta is
a man), she has never indulged in a radical physical reversal of
gender. It is true, however, that she asked Sami Frey, who has
played a lot of Latin lovers in his career, to perform a female role in
Le Théâtre de verdure, a play she wrote and which was staged by
Beno Besson in 1988. She was very enthusiastic about his
performance declaring that it was his best ever, before adding that
'chacun d'entre nous possède une part masculine et féminine,

11 'A woman can play a male role and vice versa without necessarily being
homosexual. Transvestism is not a convention of the past, it represents a form
of freedom wiped away by stupid traditions of naturalism and which we should
be capable of restoring today'.

alors pourquoi nous castrer?' (1994: 84) (each of us has a masculine and a feminine side. So why should we castrate ourselves?). In *La Belle Verte*, a sequence which was cut during the editing shows Coline Serreau playing a man in an extraordinarily convincing manner. In the same film, there is another ballet sequence when the male football team start a choreography on the pitch and the two goal-keepers end up passionately embracing and kissing each other.

Far from feminising her bisexual male characters in *Pourquoi Pas!* (which is quite an achievement in itself when one thinks that the film was released the same year as *La Cage aux folles*), Serreau provides an alternative view of the family and of the couple, with Fernand being at the same time the mother figure and the male lover of both Alex and Louis (Audé 1978: 66). The sexual community or, as Lefebvre put it, the *communisme sexuel familial* (sexual and familial communism) of *Pourquoi pas!* is a way for Serreau to challenge a model although she does not go as far as radically overturning it. By trying to abolish 'les rôles hérités' (Audé 1983: 84), she is in line with the concerns shared by many of her contemporaries regarding the family and sexual roles within it. Serreau does not necessarily dissociate relationships within the family from sexuality. She declared that: 'la sexualité qu'on a comme enfant et les rapports affectifs passionnels, qu'on entretient avec ses parents, avec ses frères, avec les gens qu'on aime, ont exactement la même nature que ceux qu'on a plus tard'[12] (Serreau 1978b: 10). This is also emphasised by her statement that: 'Le thème du ménage à trois, je suis persuadée que dans son explication psychanalytique, c'est vraiment le thème du père, de la mère et du gosse, que l'on trouve d'ailleurs dans *Pourquoi pas!* On peut retourner dans tous les sens, tous étant le père, la mère des autres'[13] (Serreau 1978a: 5). The interchanging roles within the

12 'the sexuality one has as a kid, the emotional, passionate and erotic relationships one has with parents, brothers and loved ones, all of these are of a similar nature to those one has later'.

13 'I am convinced that, from a psychoanalytical perspective, the subject of the threesome is actually about the mother, the father and the child, as can be seen in *Pourquoi pas!* As a matter of fact, this can be understood from many angles, as all the characters are the mother or the father of the others.'

family unit or familial community, with the implied mixture of sexuality and parenthood, are worth underlining as they can be found in a more negative perspective in Serreau's play *Quisaitout et Grobêta*. She linked the idea of the female lover with 'l'image de cette mère adorée et haïe, qu'on finit par tuer' (Serreau 1994: 84) (the image of the loved and hated mother whom one ends up killing).

The evolution of this desire to confront the existing and accepted functions of women throughout the 1970s, together with a reconsideration of motherhood by French feminists by the end of the 1970s, might explain the changing perspective of Serreau in *Trois hommes et un couffin*. According to Claire Duchen, 'by the end of the decade [1970s], the image of woman-as-mother, rejected in the beginning, was being reassessed rather than rejected' (1986: 51). Although Serreau did not seem to participate in the general enthusiasm regarding motherhood shared by feminists as seen earlier, she involved men in parenthood. To be more precise, she actually replaces mothers with fathers.

The 1980s: new men, new fathers, new families

By slightly altering her target in *Trois hommes et un couffin*, Serreau questions men's role within the family unit. One of the most striking choices is the quasi invisibility of women and mothers. In order to confront men with parenthood, Serreau puts the unwilling men in the position of fathers. This idea of performing gender roles is quite obvious in the film. The three male characters 'play' a mother role. Without going as far as Tania Moldeski's view that 'the film reveals men's desire to usurp women's procreative function'(1988: 70), it is true to say that none of the very few women in the film provides a conventional portrayal of motherhood. Thus we have the fleeing biological mother of the child who chooses her career rather than her child, the *vieille dame indigne*-like grandmother of the baby (performed by Marthe Villalonga, who has played many stereotypical overprotective Jewish mothers in her career) who prefers the prospect of a cruise with a female friend to baby-sitting, and the caricatural nanny from the *seconde maman* agency for whom babies are only part of the job. Left with no other alternative than to be 'surrogate mothers' themselves, since they refuse the presence of women in their household, (Pierre tells Michel when the latter suggests ringing his own mother after the discovery of the baby: 'Tu laisses les mères où elles sont. Si tu permets aux mères de s'engouffrer dans ce problème, on les a sur le dos pour dix ans. D'ailleurs c'est bien simple. Si une femme vient habiter chez nous plus d'une nuit, moi je déménage. Ca a toujours été convenu entre nous'[14]), the men are enduring the tough apprenticeship of parenthood, painfully learning that 'on ne naît pas père, on le devient'.[15] As seen in the previous chapter, and despite the claim by each that 'on a autre chose à faire dans la vie que de torcher des nourrissons',[16] they actually end up loving their new role.

More than a questioning of women's role within the family unit, Serreau seems in this film – which she considers as her most feminist one – to address the issue of the male's role in parenting. Interestingly enough, a law passed in 1984 – either just before, during or shortly after the shooting of the film – introduced the *congé parental sans distinction de sexe* (parental leave). As we have seen earlier, this is not the first time Serreau made 'social fiction'. Considering men's function as fathers does not mean that she excludes the women's part. Initially constrained within the domestic – female – space because of the baby, the three men will progressively emancipate themselves and find a rota system allowing them to work and to nurture the baby. It is worth noting, however, that Michel is seen as the most 'feminine' of the fathers. Beyond the fact that he works at home, he is the only one shown cleaning the baby's clothes, and cooking wearing a woman's apron. The feminisation of his character also affects his language

14 'Leave the mothers where they are. If you let them get involved in the problem, they'll be around pestering us for the next ten years. Anyway, let's get it straight. If a woman spends more than one night here, I'll move out. We've always agreed on that.'

15 'fathers are made and not born'; this refers to de Beauvoir's well-known assertion that 'women are made and not born'.

16 'we've more important things to do in life than to wipe a baby's arse'.

since he speaks to the baby in the same hypocoristic manner previously heard with the concierge.

However, there seems to be here an incompatibility between parenting and sexuality. By becoming 'fathers', the men – initially presented before the arrival of the baby as serial womanisers – are forced to make a vow of chastity (one actually refers to his becoming a nun – and not a monk – because of the baby). The disturbing element, though, is that the only way women are accepted back into the household in the film is when they are infantilised (see the last scene with the biological mother in a foetal position in her daughter's cradle), or as brief sexual partners. This distinction between sexuality and parenthood or motherhood is quite interesting as it could be seen as contradicting Serreau's earlier statement quoted above. In *Pourquoi pas!*, the 'performative mother' Fernand does not lose his sexual side. It also seems that the recurrent element in Serreau's films is often the opposite when women are mothers, as will be shown later.

Moreover, it is the mother's departure from the nest which triggers the crisis. From Marie's mother in *Trois hommes* and Romuald's unfaithful wife in *Romuald et Juliette*, to Victor's spouse (incidentally called Marie and performed by the actress who played the sinful Marie Magdalene in Arcand's *Jésus de Montréal*) and Victor's mother in *La Crise*, running away seems to be the only way for women to express their demands. By starting a 'strike' of their maternal duties (or for Victor's mother by deciding to 'retire' from motherhood, to liberate herself from domestic duties and be a sexual being again), Serreau's cinematographic mothers leave the men alone to confront their own inadequacies both as fathers and partners. Their invisibility within the narrative though means that women rarely have the opportunity of expressing their views on the subject. (An exception is Juliette bluntly refusing Romuald's marriage offer by giving him an inventory of his faults ... before changing her mind and marrying him while pregnant with his child.) However, their absence is often the result of unconventional solutions: thus Marie's mother abandons her child to pursue her career abroad, Juliette leaves successively the five biological fathers of her five children, Victor's wife deserts the *domicile conjugal* as does his mother, whereas his sister does not want her boyfriend to move in with her. In *La Belle Verte*, the mother (incidentally performed by Philippine Leroy-Beaulieu who played Marie's mother in *Trois hommes et un couffin*) also leaves home to think about her life after telling her husband that she stays with him for financial reasons only.

In both *Trois hommes et un couffin* and *Romuald et Juliette*, Serreau advocates an alternative family pattern to the predominant one, and this option is also different from the one in *Pourquoi pas!* There is no doubt that there was a growing concern about men's role within the family at the time, and that the cinema closely followed and expressed this tendency. Thus, in Benton's film *Kramer versus Kramer* made in 1979, the departure of the mother leaves the husband/father in the position of the carer and nurturer. In a way, Serreau did exploit the idea but it had a different echo within a French context. In a country which has always advocated a rise in the birth-rate, choosing the idea of the family (even if she 'subverts' it) was not *a priori* taking much of a risk. Let us remember here that the consensus surrounding family policy was such at the time that an advertising company could easily base its advertising campaign (meant to publicise the company) around the image of children, and cover France's walls with posters of smiling babies in 1985.

In the films Coline Serreau made in the 1980s – and she was not alone in choosing this trend – the target changed. It is no longer the couple, nor the people making up the couple, who fill the cinematographic space, it is the child. In this, Serreau has faithfully followed the times. The child becomes the one whose point of view is favoured, and this is to be found in autobiographical or semi-autobiographical accounts (see Kurys's films up to *La Baule les Pins/C'est la vie* in 1990) in the context of mainland France and in the colonial context, as Susan Hayward (1992) has emphasised.[17] Yet, the difference with the period before 1968 is that the 1980s' and 1990s' films tend to put the child at the centre of the story. In

---

17 For example, with *Chocolat* by C. Denis (1988), *Outremer* by B. Rouan (1990), or *Le Bal du gouverneur* by M.-F. Pisier (1989).

Serreau's films, not only does the child become a fundamental element of the plot, – whereas it was non-existent (in terms of visibility) in *Pourquoi pas!* – but the domestic space (women's) takes pride of place. She justifies the presence of the baby by saying that 'le bébé est un symbole ... L'histoire des rois mages, ça a toujours marché. Ici, le bébé est une fille. Signe des temps. Je ne sais pas si c'est du féminisme'[18] (1986). Furthermore, whereas the earlier film located its narrative in an 'alternative' household, the latter films take place within bourgeois, white families. However, it is true that she introduces the idea of inter-racial relations, or 'intersocial' ones. Serreau's strongly idealised sexual and social community in *Pourquoi pas!* is much watered down in what came after it. From *Trois hommes et un couffin* to *La Crise*, the director was to modify perceptibly the tone and tenor of her comedies. What is in crisis in *La Crise* is the family, and no longer just the couple. In this (family) unit, the infant reigns supreme. It is no longer a question of constructing or reinventing the couple and the relationships within it, but of organising life around the children. The wish to change the couple is apparently gone. Cocooning seems to have replaced it. The final statement of *La Crise* is summarised in the last scene where the family unit is re-created by the mother's return to the home. Daddy, mummy, a boy and a girl — it is almost an advertising image of happiness for both family and individuals. Despite a few echoes of her past beliefs, Serreau presents happiness as if it is inherent to the traditional family, seen as a closed space.

The emphasis on the family is, however, different in *Romuald et Juliette* as Juliette's family illustrates another version of Serreau's favourite subject. Although Juliette shares the screen with Romuald, it is worth noting that she is one of the rare leading female characters in Serreau's films (together with the unforgettable female ET in *La Belle Verte*), a point that will be developed later. While Juliette is often shown as a mother in the film, it is her – maternal – relationship with Romuald which prevails. It is

18 'the baby is a symbol. The story of the Three Wise Men always worked. In the film, it is a baby girl. A sign of the times. I don't know whether it is due to feminism.'

worth noting that the emphasis is very much on Juliette's household and that it is the traditional family unit (two biological parents, a son and a daughter) which seems to be in crisis, a tendency that *La Crise* confirmed. It would, however, be overoptimistic to deduce that *la famille mosaïque* is the 'solution' advocated by Serreau. She may have chosen to build the character of Juliette in order to emphasise the wide gap between her and Romuald: different social class, ethnic background and family pedigree, not forgetting her physical appearance, as far as can be from the perfect *bourgeoise* to whom Romuald is married. This is probably where she does not conform totally to her indirect model (the fairy-tale), and where she gently mocks the conventions of such a genre (this is sometimes seen as her 'feminist touch'). As mentioned earlier, Juliette shares a number of similarities with Maman Lapin (with the exception of the love-story).

The 1990s: back to family values?

If one divides Serreau's career into decades, it would be tempting to associate the films she made in the 1980s (*Trois hommes* and *Romuald et Juliette*) with the apparent death of feminism in France. In this regard, *La Crise* and *La Belle Verte*, made in 1992 and 1996 respectively, could easily be seen as a return to traditional family values at a time when post-feminism seems *de rigueur*. This does not prevent Serreau, however, continuing to question male attitudes and responses to women's expectations and desires.

In *La Crise*, it is through a series of domestic incidents he witnesses in other households that Victor is able to assess his own failures. The editing often shows shots of his face while female friends reproach their own partners for lack of support, indirectly suggesting that their criticism is valid for him as well. It is as if individual assumptions become general ones, another version perhaps of 'the personal is political'. In the same way as the three men in *Trois hommes* are offering a triple view of paternity and men's different reactions to it, the list of women's criticisms directed at men in *La Crise* transcends the boundaries of age and class. Their grievances go beyond the personal to attain the general. After the apparent failure of the *nouveaux pères* (new fathers), is Serreau following the trend of her contemporary Diane Kurys whose films (except *Coup de foudre*) can be read as a repeated admission that although men are not exactly what women might expect, the latter have to cope with them and accept their inadequacies and weaknesses? One of the most obvious differences between the two is that, unlike Kurys, Serreau, although a feminist filmmaker, does not give priority to female roles. This can be partly explained by the distinct choice of genres of the two filmmakers. Indeed, Serreau follows her male counterparts in often excluding women from her comedies. Lucy Fischer notes the bizarreness of women's excision from the genre, 'given the origins of the mode in female fertility rites'. She adds that 'where comedies are thematically "domestic", the maternal woman does appear, but she is often pernicious and peripheral to the male comic focus' (1996: 114–15). This aspect is examined in detail in Chapter 4 and it appears that there are many ambiguities in Serreau's humour. It is sometimes difficult to be sure whether women are the subjects or the objects of the joke.

Earth and alien mothers

There is, however, a film which can be seen as contradicting as well as summarising many of Serreau's previous ones (and therefore a lot of the points mentioned earlier). In *La Belle Verte,* which was her first big critical and commercial failure since 1985, she plays the leading role of a female extraterrestrial (Mila), widow and mother of five, sent to Earth to see what is going on. What could have been an interesting element (namely that she is half extraterrestrial and half earthwoman) is soon forgotten. The opening sequence which recalls Zefirelli's *Jésus de Nazareth* (1976), and which is anyway highly biblical, gives the tone. Not that we are entering the realm of religious dogma, but more that we are in the sphere of the sacred. What is sacred here is the earth which gives and produces, a wonderful metaphor for female fertility.[19] The gathering of figures resembling early Christians and their families bringing their crops emphasises the notion of an Eden-like ideal community. Although this is meant to be a joke, the most explicit biblical reference is when Mila is sent after several other space travellers including the musician Johann Sebastian Bach and Jesus, a detail which adds to the already strong Christian-inspired script. We discover the link between Mila and Christ in a scene where she enters the cathedral of Notre-Dame and recognises him on the many crucifixes which cover the walls. Mila appears then as a surprising combination of a female Messiah and Candide/Grobêta bringing peace and love to greedy and unworthy earthmen and -women, thanks to her naivety and her belief in (moral?) values. The fact that she needs babies in order to recharge her batteries (in the literal sense) could be read as another version of 'laissez venir à moi les petits enfants'. Indeed, Mila must hold babies in order to recover her spent energy. She therefore wanders around Paris in search of them. She ends up in a maternity ward where she spends the night, holding a sick baby who, as we soon learn, has been abandoned by its Croatian mother since it was the result of a rape by Serbian soldiers.

The most striking element though is the direct allusion to mothers as Madonnas. This is not new in Serreau's films as she has often used discreet references to paintings of Madonna-like figures, sometimes subverting them through a subtle gender reversal. Thus the opening sequence in *Trois hommes et un couffin* is a fixed shot of the painting of a baby, soon followed by another painting of a naked woman. The men are actually surrounded by paintings, including one in their bathroom strongly reminiscent of Lorrain's in *Qu'est-ce qu'on attend!* What is different in *La Belle Verte* is the direct showing of a series of paintings of Madonnas in the Louvre. The Madonna is by 'nature' both mother and virgin. This status of the idealised woman is a key aspect of utopia according to Jean Servier who, in his *Histoire de l'utopie*, wrote that: 'L'utopie marque l'avènement de la femme idéalisée, à la fois

---

19 One of the extras who performed in the opening sequences told me that for these scenes Serreau wanted the idea of family to be obvious from one group to the next.

vierge et mère, débarassée des soucis ménagers par les installations communautaires, libérée de la tutelle de l'homme, du père, par l'amour libre ... La mère disparaît en tant que *genitrix* [his emphasis] pour s'idéaliser en société parfaite'[20] (quoted by Audé 1978: 66).

In *Trois hommes*, the shot of Michel asleep with the baby while feeding it might confirm my previous point about 'performative gender'. Michel's long hair and baby face are quite misleading here and the choice of lighting underlines the pictorial allusion. Differently, in *Romuald et Juliette*, following the shot of Romuald (long hair) asleep amid the numerous progeny of Juliette, Juliette is shown asleep and naked in her bed in a pose reminiscent of either a sleeping beauty or a fertility goddess. The last shots of *La Crise* show Victor abandoned in his wife Mary's arms, a mixture of Madonna and recumbent effigy. This could illustrate the opposition between woman as mother and as lover (something totally absent from *La Belle Verte*). Once the female characters are mothers, this role expands to their male partners. In *Romuald et Juliette*, Romuald, when declaring his love to Juliette, tells her: 'Vous êtes la mère que j'aurais voulu avoir et la fille que je voudrais protéger. J'ai jamais fait l'amour avec personne comme avec vous'.[21] In *La Crise*, when the mother (Maria Pacôme) announces her departure from home and gives a list of her claims, she declares: 'Pendant trente ans je vous ai torchés, nourris, couchés, consolés ... tous les trois'[22] – the three being Victor, his sister Isabelle and their father.

Conclusion

Despite questionable and sometimes ambiguous representations of womanhood and motherhood, Coline Serreau seems to be giving more and more power to her female characters as mothers.

20 'Utopia shows the advent of the idealised woman, both virgin and mother, freed from domestic duties thanks to the communal organisations, freed from men's and fathers' guidance thanks to free love ... The mother figure disappears as a *genitrix* to be idealised in a perfect society.'
21 'You are the mother I wish I had and the daughter I would like to protect. I have never made love like that before.'
22 'For the last thirty years, I wiped, fed, cradled, consoled all three of you.'

Although it could be argued that women's control in the domestic sphere is a typical and recurrent trend in patriarchal societies such as France, her films and plays nonetheless try to show how power relationships go beyond gender and are also class- and race-related. In this regard, families as a microcosm of society as a whole could become the space where changes can initially occur. For Serreau, motherhood is also a formidable strength for women since they have the power to create life. The despair of Jacques, Marie's father in *Trois hommes et un couffin*, who pretends to be pregnant, is echoed in the final monologue of Maman Lapin. She addresses both sexes: 'A vous les hommes, je dis pliez, devenez ronds, laissez la connaissance vous submerger ... N'ayez pas le désespoir de vos ventres à jamais vides d'enfants'.[23] To women, she declares: 'Femmes, celui qui ne veut pas voir qui vous êtes, combattez-le avec violence, femmes, que celles d'entre vous qui laissent encore les hommes faire leurs meurtres soient maudites et crèvent dans la poussière, car le monde qui est à l'ordre du jour ne pourra pas se faire sans vous'.[24]

References

Audé, F. (1978), 'Aujourd'hui et demain: *Mais qu'est-ce qu'elles veulent?* et *Pourquoi pas!*', *Positif*, no. 203, January, pp. 63–6.

Audé, F. (1981), *Ciné-modèle, cinéma d'elles*, Lausanne, L'Age d'Homme.

Audé, F. (1983), 'Métamorphoses du couple et glissements progressifs vers l'utopie', *CinémAction*, no. 25, pp. 80–9.

Bard, C. (1995), *Les Filles de Marianne: histoire des féminismes 1914–1940*, Paris, Fayard.

Burch, N. and Sellier, G. (1996), *La Drôle de guerre des sexes du cinéma français 1930–1956*, Paris, Nathan Université.

Duchen, C. (1986), *Feminism in France: From May '68 to Mitterrand*, London, Routledge.

Duchen, C. (1994), *Women's Rights and Women's Lives in France 1944–1968*, London and New York, Routledge.

23 'To you men, I say, bend a bit, become round, let knowledge overwhelm you. Don't be made desperate by your empty wombs.'

24 'Women, fight aggressively against he who does not want to accept who you are, women, a curse on those of you who still allow men to commit murders, may you die like dogs. For the new world to come cannot exist without you.'

Fischer, L. (1996), *Cinematernity: Film, Motherhood, Genre*, Princeton, Princeton University Press.

Fortino, S. (1997), 'De filles en mères: la seconde vague du féminisme et la maternité', *Clio. Femmes, Histoire et Société*, no. 5, pp. 217–38.

Hayward, S. (1992), 'Women filmmakers in the 1980s: now you see them, now you don't', unpublished paper given at the Conference on Women in French cinema, at the University of Birmingham.

Kaplan, E. A. (1992), *Motherhood and Representation: The Mother in Popular Culture and Melodrama*, London and New York, Routledge.

Leclerc, A. (1974), *Parole de femme*, Paris, Grasset.

Modleski, T. (1988), 'Three men and baby M', *Camera Obscura*, May, pp. 69–81.

Rémy, M. (1990), *De l'utopie à l'intégration: histoire des mouvements des femmes*, Paris, L'Harmattan.

Ringart, N. (1991), 'Quand ce n'était qu'un dé but ... Itinéraires de femmes à Paris', in *Crises de la société, féminisme et changements*, Paris, Editions Tierce.

Rollet, B. (1997), 'Two women filmmakers speak out: Serreau and Balasko and the inheritance of May '68', in *Voices of France*, S. Perry and M. Cross (eds), London and Washington, Pinter, pp. 100–13.

Serreau, C. (1978a), 'Coline Serreau: la force des convictions et le plaisir du spectacle', interview in *Jeune Cinéma*, no. 110, April–May, pp. 1–7.

Serreau, C. (1978b), 'Coline Serreau: à propos de son film: *Mais qu'est-ce qu'elles veulent?*', interview in *Des Femmes en Mouvement*, February, pp. 9–10.

Serreau, C. (1978c), 'Coline Serreau: une contestataire tranquille', interview in *La Revue du Cinéma: Image et Son*, no. 325, February, pp. 27–9.

Serreau, C. (1982), interview in *Le Quotidien de Paris*, 2 September.

Serreau, C. (1986), 'Coline Serreau: à l'école des grands', interview in *Le Monde*, 2 January.

Serreau, C. (1994), 'Coline Serreau: parce que la vie n'est pas si grave', interview in *Télérama*, no. 2341, 23 November, pp. 83–4.

Conclusion

From rebellion to consensus or vice versa?

When I asked Coline Serreau the question which opens this conclusion, she objected to the word consensus, claiming that she had
not stopped what she started more than two decades ago. Indeed,
she still feels very strongly about her initial beliefs and thinks that
her work still conveys them. Besides her films, the stage appears
to have become for her a platform where she can continue to
express her desire for change. When, talking about feminism, she
mentioned *Trois hommes et un couffin* – perceived by French
audiences and by many critics as a feminist comedy – the gap
between the French and the Anglo-Saxon receptions and percep-
tions of her work seems extremely wide. Without analysing this
point in detail, I would prefer to focus on the wider issue of
women in contemporary French cinema from the mid-1980s
onwards.

In the conclusion of her book on *French Women's Writing 1848–
1994*, Diana Holmes emphasises the dilemma women writers
were confronted with and which many women filmmakers in
France have encountered in their career. They had and still have to
choose between, on the one hand, integration and assimilation
into a patriarchal system (in other words the reluctance to be
called women writers or women filmmakers and to accept a
gendered conception of their work), and on the other hand, the
rejection of 'the assimilationist model of feminism in the name of

a more radical challenge to patriarchy, choosing to stay "on the margins" in order to develop an alternative philosophy based on their feminine difference' (1996: 267). Where film is concerned, there has not been a real equivalent of the *écriture féminine* advocated by some feminist writers from the 1970s, despite attempts by the contributors of *Paroles ... elles tournent*. However, just as there are genres considered in literature as 'female', it was until recently easy to identify a tendency for women filmmakers to make a certain sort of film. What predominated in the critics' terminology in the 1980s was the use of the adjective *intimiste* (intimist) when referring to women's films. Indeed, the recurrent choice of autobiography by female directors indirectly called for such labelling. However, the way their films – whether they were 'intimist' or not – were received called into question the criteria on which they were judged and assessed. Similarly, the recurrent omission of female directors from recent French publications dedicated to the history of French cinema says a lot about the consideration (or more precisely in this case the lack of consideration) of their work. There is little doubt that Holmes's comments and questions regarding women writers in France could easily be transposed to female filmmakers, and I purposely 'misquote' her:

> Even in the last two decades, with huge increases in both the number and the visibility of women-authored texts, female, and particularly feminist [directors] tend to be ghettoised as a separate, minority category ... Has [directing] been a largely male domain? Were they [women] entirely caught up in the ideological web that constructed them as man's Other? Or is it, rather, that the process of selection and evaluation has written women out of the canon, judging them against criteria which identified serious concerns with male concerns? (Holmes 1996: xii)

In the 1970s and 1980s women's films were largely seen as reproducing the dichotomy between the external world traditionally associated with the 'masculine' and the domestic, 'feminine' sphere, dealing with issues such as sexuality, motherhood and family, and often confining their narratives and characters within a restricted geographical space. The huge difficulties most women filmmakers faced (and many still do) to finance their films meant that, when they could find a producer, they were (are), willingly or not, reduced to making cheaper films than their male counterparts. Despite her established reputation as a successful filmmaker, Coline Serreau could not find a producer to support her project for a silent film called *Chari-Bohu* in 1990. The actress-turned-director Brigitte Rouan, whose autobiographical film *Outremer* was praised by the critics when it was released in 1990 (with the award of the Semaine de la Critique in Cannes the same year), had to struggle for seven years before being able to finance her second film *Post coïtum, animal triste* released in September 1997. She eventually made it without a producer and had to create her own production company. As she played the female leading role in both films, it was tempting to read her film, a passionate love-affair between a married middle-class 40-year-old woman and a young man in his twenties, as another autobiographical text. Beyond the categorisation of the film, it seems quite probable that she was confronted with discrimination based on the one hand on her sex and on the other on her background as an actress. The actress-director Nicole Garcia encountered similar problems when she made her second film, *Le Fils préféré*, in 1994. After a first film, *Un Week-end sur deux* (1990), dealing with 'women's issues' such as divorce and motherhood, the main protagonists of *Le Fils préféré* were male. Questions then arose about the ability of a woman – especially for someone like Nicole Garcia who otherwise complies with the unwritten rules of femininity and the classic aesthetic criteria in France – to make a 'buddy movie'.[1] The same things happened when Serreau made *Trois hommes et un couffin* and some critics were eager to know what it was like for a man like André Dussolier to be directed by a woman with such a feminist reputation.

If one keeps in mind the unofficial restrictions regarding the filmic genres available to women, one could wonder whether by choosing a traditionally 'male' genre some women directors were not perceived as 'marginalising' themselves from the accepted

1 At the end of 1997 Garcia was shooting *Place Vendôme* with Catherine Deneuve.

notion of 'what a woman [director] should do'.[2] Since *Pas très catholique* by Tonie Marshall (1994), a detective story starring Anémone as the female detective, and *Personne ne m'aime*, a female road movie directed by Marion Vernoux in 1994, some female directors have tended to opt for other cinematographic genres. Despite the overwhelming majority of comedies directed by male directors, with mostly male protagonists, there is a less and less timid reappropriation of the genre by a few female directors who provide actresses with leading female roles.[3] There is also some progress – albeit minimal – in other traditionally male cinematographic areas. The recent release of *Artemisia* by Agnès Merlet (1997) and *Marquise* by Véra Belmont (1997),[4] two costume dramas set in the seventeenth century, both directed by women filmmakers and with strong female leading parts, could be read as a sign that even a male-dominated genre such as the heritage film is now accessible to female directors.

More important perhaps is the emergence of filmmakers coming from outside the traditional film circles, whose social and ethnic background contrast with their elders'. Thus, the release in 1995 of the first film made by the *beurette* Zaïda Ghorab-Volta,[5] *Souviens-toi de moi*, brought a much needed feminine element to what is now called 'beur cinema' and in which the absence of female protagonists was, until recently, a recurrent feature. The success of *Y aura-t-il de la neige à Noël?*, the first film by the unknown and young film neophyte Sandrine Veysset in 1996, illustrates this trend. It also shows that the 'feminisation' of French cinema seems to go beyond the increasing number of female directors within the French film industry. Even if these signs should be viewed with caution, they are nonetheless evidence that things are changing. Another confirmation of this tendency is the growing

2 In another context, the American female director Katherine Bigelow faced similar reactions after each of her films which did not fit with what the audience and critics expected from a woman director. The issue was fuelled when her last film, *Strange Days*, was released in 1995.

3 See, for example, Josiane Balasko, Valérie Lemercier and Dominique Giacobbi.

4 Her first film, *Rouge Baiser* made in 1985 and set during the Cold War, could be seen as a heritage film as well.

5 This is the feminine equivalent of *beur*.

interest that these films seem now to attract from critics and audience alike. On the eve of the twenty-first century, one can only hope that these female directors' films will have the power to reverse sexual stereotypes and to fulfil the wish film director Nelly Kaplan expressed in 1976: 'Mais de grâce, que les films faits par des femmes soient construits pour intéresser – même en dérangeant, surtout en dérangeant – tout le monde! Il s'agit de raconter des histoires. Et à travers elles, de détrôner ce qui est le poison le plus insidieux du cinéma: sa misogynie'[6] (p. 14). There is very little doubt that Serreau has greatly contributed to such a fight in the past twenty years.

References

Holmes, D. (1996), *French Women's Writing 1848–1994*, London and Atlantic Highlands, Athlone.

Kaplan, N. (1976), 'A nous l'histoire d'une de nos folies', in *Paroles … elles tournent*, des femmes de Musidora, Paris, Editions des Femmes, p. 14.

6 'But please, let's make sure that women's films hold interest for everyone, even and especially if they are disturbing. We should tell stories, and through them we must expel the most insidious poison in cinema: its misogyny.'

Filmography

This filmography also includes television and theatre work.

Serreau as film director

Mais qu'est-ce qu'elles veulent?, 1975–78

90 minutes, col.
Production Company: Copra films/INA
Script: Coline Serreau
Camera: Jean-François Robin
Editing: Sophie Tatischeff, Joëlle Hache, Françoise Collin
Sound: Coline Serreau
Music: Johann Sebastian Bach
Documentary
Selection Cannes Festival 1977 in section 'L'Air du Temps'
Broadcast on French TV: 1982

Pourquoi pas!, 1977

93 minutes, col.
Production Company: Dimage/SND
Executive Producer: Michèle Dimitri
Production Manager: Michèle Dimitri
Assistant Directors: Patrick Dewolf, Georges Manulelis, Roch Stephanik
Script: Coline Serreau
Camera: Jean-François Robin
Editing: Sophie Tatischeff
Continuity: Anne Mirman

Sound: Alain Lachassagne
Music: Jean-Pierre Mas
Location: Villiers sur Marne (Paris suburb)
Awards: Georges Sadoul's, *Elle*'s readers
Principal actors: Sami Frey (Fernand), Mario Gonzalez (Louis), Christine Murillo (Alex), Nicole Jamet (Sylvie), Michel Aumont (the police inspector), Marthe Souberbie (Sylvie's mother)

Qu'est-ce qu'on attend pour être heureux!, 1982

92 minutes, col.
Production Company: Elephant Production/UGC/Top 1
Executive Producer: Michèle Dimitri
Production Manager: Raymond Danon
Assistant Directors: Elisabeth Parnière, Anne-Marie Gamet, James Canal
Script: Coline Serreau
Camera: Jean-Noël Ferragut
Editing: Jacqueline Meppiel
Continuity: Anne Mirman
Sound: Pierre Gamet
Music: Jeff Cohen
Art Direction: Jean Galland
Costumes: Edith Vesperini
Make-up: Anne-Marie Martiquet
Location: Villiers sur Marne (Paris suburb)
Principal actors: Romain Bouteille (Joachim), Evelyne Buyle (Jean Harlow), Henri Garcin (the film director), André Gille (Maurice), Pierre Vernier (Rudolph Valentino), Marthe Souverbie (Nini)

Trois hommes et un couffin, 1985

106 minutes, col.
Production Company: Flash Films/Soprofilm/TF1 Films Production
Executive Producer: Jean-François Lepetit
Production Managers: Jacques Attia, Henri Viart
Assistant Directors: Graziella Molinaro, Dominique Chaulot Talmon, Pierre de Rivière
Script: Coline Serreau
Camera: Jean-Yves Escoffier, Jean-Jacques Bouhon
Editing: Catherine Renault
Continuity: Ariane Litaize, Christine Broustet Lepetit

Sound: Daniel Ollivier
Music: Schubert, Rostropovitch
Art Direction: Jacques Maussion
Costumes: Edith Vesperini, Poussine Mercanton
Make-up: Anne Bourdiol
Location: Paris
Awards: 3 Césars 1985 – best film, best script, best support role for
    Michel Boujenah
Principal actors: Michel Boujenah (Michel), André Dussollier (Jacques),
    Roland Giraud (Pierre), Dominique Lavanant (Madame Rapon),
    Philippine Leroy Beaulieu (Sylvia), Marthe Villalonga (Jacques's
    mother)

Romuald et Juliette, 1989

108 minutes, col.
Production Company: Cinéa/FR3 Films
Executive Producers: Jean-Louis Piel, Philippe Carcassonne
Production Managers: Catherine Leray, Philippe Savournin
Assistant Director: Pierre Abela
Script: Coline Serreau
Camera: Jean-Noël Ferragut
Editing: Catherine Renault
Continuity: Ariane Litaize
Sound: Philippe Lioret, Gérard Lamps
Music: Duke Ellington, James Cotton, Aconio Dolo, etc.
Art Direction: Jean-Marc Stehle
Costumes: Monique Perrot
Make-up: Michel Deruelle
Location: Paris and suburbs
Principal actors: Daniel Auteuil (Romuald Blindet), Firmine Richard
    (Juliette Bonaventure), Pierre Vernier (Blache), Maxime Leroux
    (Cloquet), Gilles Privat (Paulin), Catherine Salviat (Françoise)

Contre l'oubli, 1991

3 minutes (total film: 90 minutes), col. and b/w
Production Company: Amnesty International
Broadcast on French TV: November–December 1991

La Crise, 1992

108 minutes, col.
Production Company: Les Films Alain Sarde/TF1 Films Production/
Leader Cinematografica/Raidue/Canal+
Executive Producer: Alain Sarde
Production Manager: Claude Albouze
Assistant Director: Elisabeth Parnière, Clauss Gigli, Laurent Soulet
Script: Coline Serreau
Camera: Bruno Privat
Editing: Catherine Renault
Continuity: Catherine Prévert
Sound: Boris Viard, Sophie Durand
Music: Sonia Wieder-Atherton
Art Direction: Robert Alazraki
Costumes: Karen Muller, Nathalie Cercuel
Make-up: Joël Lavau, Nathalie Louichon
Location: Paris and the Alps
Awards: César 1993 for best script
Principal actors: Vincent Lindon (Victor), Patrick Timsit (Michou),
Zabou (Isabelle), Maria Pacôme (Victor's mother), Yves Robert
(Victor's father), Michèle Laroque (Martine)

La Belle Verte, 1996

108 minutes, col.
Production Company: Les Films Alain Sarde/TF1 Films Production/
Canal+
Executive Producer: Alain Sarde
Production Manager: Gérard Crosnier
Assistant Directors: Catherine Puentas, Elisabeth Parnière, Laurent
Soulet
Script: Coline Serreau
Camera: Robert Alazraki
Editing: Catherine Renault
Continuity: Catherine Prévert, Zoé Zurstrassen, Bérangère Cros
Sound: Guillaume Sciama, Dominique Dalmasso
Music: Coline Serreau
Art Direction: Robert Alazraki
Costumes: Karen Muller
Make-up: Nathalie Tissier
Location: Paris, Auvergne, Lozère and Australia

Principal actors: Coline Serreau (Mila), Vincent Lindon (Max), Paul Crauchet (Osam), Philippine Leroy Beaulieu (Florence), Samuel Tasinaje (Mesaul), James Thieree (Mesaje)

L'Enfant, 1998

Part of *Lumière sur un massacre*
3 minutes (total film: 30 minutes), col.
Production Company: Little Bear (for Handicap International)
Broadcast on French TV: November–December 1997
Project awarded the 1997 Nobel Prize (with all the international associations involved in fighting the use of landmines)

Serreau as film actor

Un peu, beaucoup, passionnément, 1970
Director: Robert Enrico

Dada au cœur, 1972
Director: Claude Accursi (not released)

On s'est trompé d'histoire d'amour, 1974
Director: Jean-Louis Bertuccelli
Script and dialogues: Coline Serreau

Sept morts sur ordonnance, 1975
Director: Jacques Rouffio

Le Fou de Mai, 1977
Director: Philippe Defrance

La Belle Verte, 1996
Director: Coline Serreau

Serreau and television

Pont dormant, 1972
Director: F. Marzèle
(Coline Serreau as actor)

Le Rendez-vous, 1975
Director: Coline Serreau
2nd channel
(short fiction)

Grand-mères de l'Islam, 1978
Director: Coline Serreau
1st channel and INA
(documentary)
Broadcast on French TV: Summer 1980

Oedipe roi, 1980
Director: Coline Serreau
RAI (Italian TV)
Repeat of a show directed by Beno Besson

Serreau and theatre

Molière and Farce, 1966
Tour with Dominique Serreau (Coline's brother) and the Companie
    des Sept.
Acting and music

Contraceptivement vôtre, 1967
Playwright and director: Didier Kaminka

La Guerre de Troie n'aura pas lieu, 1969
Playwright: Jean Giraudoux
Trainee
Venue: Comédie Française

L'Escalier de Silas, 1970
Playwright: Geneviève Serreau
Leading role
Venue: Théâtre du Vieux-Colombier (Paris)

Amédée, 1970
Playwright: Ionesco
Director: Jean-Marie Serreau
Théâtre de Poche (Paris)

Thérèse est triste, 1971
Playwright: Coline Serreau with Coluche
Director: Coluche
Leading role
Venue: Théâtre du Vieux-Colombier

Un Petit nid d'amour, 1971
Playwright: Georges Michel
Director: Alain Scoff

Le Songe d'une nuit d'été (Shakespeare's *A Midsummer Night's Dream*), 1971
Director: Jean Gyllibert
Festival of Chateauvallon

Le Soir des diplomates, 1973
Playwright: Romain Bouteille
Director: Romain Bouteille
Venue: Théâtre de Poche (Paris)

Liola (from Pirandello), 1973
Director: Gabriel Garrand

Othello (Shakespeare's *Othello*), 1974
Director: Stephane Meldegg
Role: Desdemona
Venue: Festival du Marais (Paris)

Citrouille, 1975
Playwright: Jean Barbaud
Director: Dominique Serreau
Venue: Théâtre de la Tempête (Paris)

Comme il vous plaira (Shakespeare's *As You Like It*), 1976
Director: Beno Besson
Role: Rosalinde
Festival d'Avignon
Festival de l'Est Parisien (Paris)

Le Cercle de craie caucasien (Brecht's *The Caucasian Chalk Circle*), 1977
Playwright: Bertolt Brecht
Director: Beno Besson
Leading role

Lapin Lapin, 1986
Playwright: Coline Serreau, under the pseudonym of Elie Bourquin
Director: Beno Besson
Leading role
Venue: Théâtre de la Ville (Paris)

Le Dragon, 1987
Playwright: Eugeni Schwarz
Director: Beno Besson
Leading role
Venue: Théâtre de la Ville (Paris)

Le Théâtre de verdure, 1988
Playwright and director: Beno Besson
Leading role

Quisaitout et Grobêta, 1993
Playwright: Coline Serreau
Director: Beno Besson
Leading role
Venue: Théâtre de la Place Saint Martin (Paris)
Awards: 4 Molières: Best comic play, best director for Beno Besson,
    best costume designer and best set designer
(text published by Actes Sud-Papiers, 1993)

Moi un homme ancien marin, 1994–95
Playwright: Coline Serreau

Voyage ou l'agonie d'un jeune homme, 1996–97
Playwright: Coline Serreau

Le Salon d'été, 1998
Playwright: Coline Serreau
Director: Coline Serreau
Leading role
Venue: Théâtre de l'Europe (Paris)

Select bibliography

Publications on French women filmmakers and French women's history

Audé, F. *Ciné-modèle, cinéma d'elles*, Lausanne, L'Age d'Homme, 1981. One of the rare books devoted to women and films in France which dedicates a chapter to Coline Serreau.

Avant-Scène Cinéma, 'Trois hommes et un couffin', no. 356, January 1987. Issue devoted to the film, with script, stills, interview and background articles.

Avant-Scène Cinéma, 'La Crise', no. 468, January 1998. Issue devoted to the film, with script, stills, interview and background articles.

CinémAction, '1960–1980: vingt ans d'utopie au cinéma', M. Serceau (ed.), no. 25, 1983. One article on *Pourquoi pas!*

CinémAction, 'Le Cinéma au féminisme', no. 31, 1985. Many references to Serreau's work.

CinémAction, 'Le Documentaire français', R. Piédal (ed.), no. 41, 1987. One article on *Mais qu'est-ce qu'elles veulent?*

CinémAction, 'Le Comique à l'écran', no. 82, 1997. Several articles on French comedy.

Colvile, G. 'On Coline Serreau's *Mais qu'est-ce qu'elles veulent?* And the problematics of feminist documentary', *French Cinema*, R. King (ed.), Nottingham French Studies, vol. 32, no. 1, Spring 1993, pp. 84–9. Analysis of Serreau's documentary.

Duchen, C. *Feminism in France: From May '68 to Mitterrand*, London, Routledge, 1986. A major study of women and feminism in France from the Second World War.

Duchen, C. (ed.), *French Connections: Voices from the Women's Movement in France*, London, Hutchinson, 1987. A major study of women and feminism in France from the Second World War.

Duchen, C. *Women's Rights and Women's Lives in France 1944–1968*, London and New York, Routledge, 1994. A major study of women and feminism in France from the Second World War.

Flitterman-Lewis, S. *To Desire Differently: Feminism and the French Cinema*, Urbana and Chicago, University of Illinois Press, 1990. Although this book does not deal directly with Serreau, it provides a very good introduction to the subject of women and film making in France.

Lejeune, P. *Le Cinéma des femmes*, Paris, Lherminier, 1987. One of the rare books devoted to women and films in France, which dedicates an entry to Coline Serreau.

Musidora (des femmes de), *Paroles ... elles tournent*, Paris, Editions des Femmes, 1976. A collection of essays and testimonies from French female filmmakers, including texts by Serreau herself.

Overbey, D, 'France: the Newest Wave', *Sight and Sound*, Spring 1978, pp. 87–8. Interview with Coline Serreau.

Rollet, B. 'Two women filmmakers speak out: Serreau and Balasko and the inheritance of May '68', in *Voices of France*, S. Perry and M. Cross (eds), London and Washington, Pinter, 1997, pp. 100–13. Analysis of Serreau's evolution from 1975 onwards with regard to May '68.

Serceau, D. 'Les Jeux de la vérité et du mensonge au service du "bien"', *CinémAction*, no. 41, 1987, pp. 88–105. Analysis of Serreau's documentary *Mais qu'est-ce qu'elles veulent?*

Serreau, C. *Quisaitout et Grobêta*, Paris, Actes Sud-Papiers, 1993.

Dossier Coline Serreau, Bibliothèque Marguerite Durand, Paris.

Siclier, J. *La Femme dans le cinéma français*, Paris, Editions du Cerf, 1957. Analysis of women in the French cinema of the Fourth Republic.

Vincendeau, G. (ed.) 'Women as auteur-e-s: notes from Créteil', *Screen*, XXVII: 3–4, 1986, pp. 156–62. Report from the Créteil Women Film Festival.

Vincendeau, G. 'Women's cinema, film theory and feminism in France', *Screen*, XXVIII: 4, 1987, pp. 4–18. Report from the Créteil Women Film Festival in the wider context of women, feminism and films in France.

Vincendeau, G. 'Créteil 1988: ten years on', *Screen*, XXIX: 4, 1988, pp. 128–32. Report from the Créteil Women Film Festival after the celebration of the 10th festival.

Vincendeau, G. 'Less players, some celebration', *Sight and Sound*, II: 3, July 1992, p. 5. Créteil Women Film Festival report.

Vincendeau, G. 'Hijacked: war of attrition', *Sight and Sound*, III: 7, July 1993, pp. 22–5. Article on Hollywood remakes of French films, dealing with the cultural obstacles to remakes and the financial aspect.

Vincendeau, G. 'Coline Serreau: a high wire act', *Sight and Sound*, IV: 3, March 1994, pp. 26–8. Article devoted to Coline Serreau and the way she deals with the issue of gender in her films; it also provides information on French comedy and women's input to the genre.

Interviews with Coline Serreau

'Coline Serreau: la force des convictions et le plaisir du spectacle', *Jeune Cinéma*, no. 110, April–May 1978, pp. 1–7.

'Coline Serreau: à propos de son film: *Mais qu'est-ce qu'elles veulent?*', *Des Femmes en Mouvement*, February 1978, pp. 9–10.

'Planer ... Coline au trapèze', *Des Femmes en Mouvement*, February 1978, pp. 12–13.

'Coline Serreau: une contestataire tranquille', *La Revue du Cinéma: Image et Son*, no. 325, February 1978, pp. 27–9.

'Entretien avec Coline Serreau', *Cinématographe*, July 1982, pp. 21–3.

'Coline Serreau: parce que la vie n'est pas si grave', *Télérama*, no. 2341, 23 November 1994, pp. 83–4.

Index